Unforeseen Exit

When you find yourself facing divorce
& suddenly single

Keli Hazel

Paperback ISBN	978-1-922740-10-6
Hardback ISBN	978-1-922740-11-3
Digital ISBN	978-1-922740-12-0

Unforeseen Exit

When you find yourself facing divorce & suddenly single

Keli Hazel

Dedication

I dedicate this book to my three incredible young men Matt, Michael, and Mitch. You are my heart and soul: my inspiration, my purpose, and my loves. Raising you three has molded me into a better version of myself.

Love you to the moon and back!

Thank you

Many people inspired me through this journey. They trusted, supported, and loved me not only while I was writing this book, but during that ugly, tumultuous time when I went through my divorce.

I would like to thank my girlfriends Brenda, Lisa, Melissa, and Michele who were there every step of the way: through all the tears, anger, and eventually laughter. Thank you for all the hugs, pep talks, and support.

I would also like to thank Karen for her spiritual guidance, and Bennet, the first man whom I let into my life after everything. He was my best friend for many years, and we were the voice of reason and encouragement for each other. I would also like to thank a creative, fun-loving and caring man whom I dated for many years, Ron. You taught me so much and inspired me, more than you know.

There are a handful of ladies who are in my corner today and I know they will always be. Katie, Linda, and Mary, you are my cheerleaders, protectors, sounding boards, and more importantly, my friends for life.

Thanks to a lady —whose name I prefer to keep to myself— whom I believe God placed in my life specifically because our lives parallel each other.

Love you all!

I would be remiss if I did not thank the lady who encouraged, inspired, and directed me the most in writing this book, my book coach. At our first meeting, I thought there was no way I could write a book: I am a left-brained girl who is analytical all the way. English Language and creative writing classes have never been my thing. But she was kind, empathetic, honest, and kept me on track. Not only was she my book coach but she was my confidant and therapist whenever I hit an emotional roadblock.

Thank you, Paulette!

And to the rest of you whose names aren't included here, please be assured that you all are in my heart. I am forever grateful!

Introduction

There always have been two sides to every story.

This is my side of the story: how I felt, what I went through, and how I became a better person as a result.

Do you feel alone, confused, and overwhelmed? Has your life suddenly taken a different path than you had planned? Are your dreams being shattered into a thousand pieces? Do you feel like the proverbial rug has been pulled out from under your feet?

Well, I have been there.

In an effort to reduce your feelings of loneliness as much as possible, I will give you some guidance by sharing my story. And I will be transparent and vulnerable so as to help you through this tumultuous time in your life, hopefully.

Hello to those who are contemplating becoming single again or those who have become single all of a sudden. Here is my jumping-off point, where I ask myself several difficult questions. Question related to the reasons behind this book you are holding in your hands. For me to articulate my why, what, who, and how, I had to ask myself several questions.

Why did I write this book? What did I have to share that others haven't already heard of?

What was I hoping to accomplish with this book?

Who do I want to help?

And how can this book help them?

Let's go back in time to 2003 – 2004. This was when it felt like my husband suddenly started pulling away from me and our boys. When I say suddenly, I mean a complete 180-degree turn. We just had our third child, and he was being the model father and husband. Then in February 2003, I felt like he checked out on us. I did not know what was going on. He no longer behaved like the man I married. I felt like my marriage was heading downhill right before my eyes, and I had absolutely no clue why.

I do not consider myself a writer and I was not one of those women who wrote journals during their adulthood or kept diaries as a teenager. However, when I had no idea what was happening to my marriage and I confided in a good friend of mine, she suggested that I start a journal. Taking her advice, I started writing down everything I went through right from the beginning of my "summer of hell" as I call it, all the way through my divorce process and until it was finalized, and for a while after.

Now fast forward to 2007, I had this overwhelming desire to help women. So, I reached out to a local domestic violence shelter and asked how I could be of help. I have been an advocate of this organization ever since.

That same year, I came up with an idea of how to help women keep their jewelry safe, organized, and easily accessible while traveling. That was what led to the birth of my company, Keli's Kreations, LLC. I took my idea from just that, an idea, to market. But this was not quite what I had in mind —I wanted to make a difference, to help women. But I didn't know how.

For as long as I can remember, I have been religious —I believed in God, went to church regularly, and tried to be a good person. But looking back, I realized that despite being religious and a regular church goer, I never had a personal relationship with God. I believe God saw that and did not like where I was headed. And I'm sure that was why everything I knew and a large part of who I was changed during my "summer of hell."

It was not an overnight change by any means; it was, and still is, a journey. And I know without any doubt that God wants me to be vulnerable and share my story. It wasn't the right time when my children were young but, now is the time. It's scary to be vulnerable but if I can help at least one person navigate through a time as tumultuous as going through a divorce, then it is well worth it.

This desire to help women led me to pick up my journals — which I had not touched since my divorce was finalized in 2004— in the fall of 2007. From the beginning of my marital issues until divorce, I filled up four journals. It was definitely helpful back then and going through them for a second time has been empowering and therapeutic.

Please don't get me wrong, I am not implying that it didn't lead me to getting upset or stirring up past emotions —it actually led me to reliving those difficult moments.

Everyone's story is different and unique in some way, but many of them are similar in terms of feelings, experiences, and difficulties. I had this overwhelming desire to share my story, but I always thought, *was this the right time?*

Years ago, I tried. But then, I had nine-, seven-, and five-year-olds. Life was busy and not a lot of quiet time was left for me. Raising three kids on my own wasn't an easy feat, but I am not complaining at all. I would not trade the time that I had staying home and raising my boys for anything in the world. It was priceless!

So, who am I?

I am Keli Jo Hinchliffe. I was born and bred in Ft. Lauderdale, Florida, to Robert and Jeanne Hinchliffe: two loving, hardworking parents who knew how to be content with the little they had. My dad was in the grocery business. He started as a meat cutter and worked his way up to store manager. And my mother was a full-time housewife who devoted all she had to caring for and supporting her family.

She was one of nine children, and her family was a blended one as she lost her father to black lung disease when she was nine. He was a coal miner in Pennsylvania who had come over from Naples, Italy on a boat right into Ellis Island.

I am the third of four children. My two older sisters are ten and eleven years older than I am, and my brother is four years younger. My mother says she always wanted four boys. Well with me being the third girl my mother likes to tell the story of when she had me, that the doctor joked, "it's another girl...let's put her back." I was not the easiest baby. My mother and sisters say I cried for a year straight. They used to take turns rocking me and walking me around. I was quite the pain, I'm sure.

Like most little girls, I had dreams and aspirations. All I wanted to do was dance on Broadway and eventually marry my prince charming. I wanted to have four children, live in a house with a white picket fence, and have a golden retriever. From a very young age until way into my twenties, my whole life was centered on my dancing. I started dancing at the age of three, though I was not eager to at that age as I was painfully shy and the kind of child who always hid behind her mother's legs if a stranger, or anyone for that matter, approached her. My mother thought that dancing might help bring me out of my shell. Boy, was she right!

I grew up to become a determined, disciplined, and somewhat stubborn go-getter. I must admit that I was wound up pretty tight in my younger years, definitely a type A personality. Maybe even a bit obsessive at times. I often wonder why I was so uptight or *anal retentive* as I used to say back then. It was a result of heredity, environmental influence, or circumstances, I suppose.

I'm telling you all this because I am just an average person who lived an average life. I am not clairvoyant and definitely not perfect. I do not have a magic wand with which I can fix every problem, neither do I have all the answers. I cannot answer the question of why I went through a divorce with 100 percent certainty. What I do know is that I am going to be vulnerable with you by sharing my story.

I promise to be open-minded, honest, and genuine with you.

I lived through one of the most traumatic experiences anyone could ever go through —a divorce. When I stood in front of the preacher and said my vows to the hearing of my family and friends, I meant for good or for bad; I promised to be all in.

To have broken those vows was difficult to get over.

But you know what? I got through it! With lots of support, determination, sacrifice, and prayers, I got through it. I won't lie to you by passing off everything I went through as easy, because it most definitely was not. I shed tears for days on end, filled up many journals, took counseling classes via Divorce Care, learned how to set new boundaries, participated in Bible studies, and read the Bible daily on my own. Though many years have gone by and the feelings and bad memories have faded, they haven't completely gone away. However, I can say with everything in me that I am in a better place as a result of my experience.

Did I want this? No. Was this what I planned for myself and my boys? No, again. One thing I can say yes to though, is that God plucked me out of my marriage because He did not like who I was turning into. I didn't like me either. He took me on a journey I believe I am still on, a journey that made me the mother, woman, daughter, sister, aunt, and friend that He wanted me to be. I believe we are all a work in progress in one way or another, and I am no exception. *But girl, I have come so far.* And so can you! I want to walk with you and be that person you can lean on and relate to during this tumultuous time in your life. So, at the end of each chapter, I share the advice I've learned from women I've interviewed in the *You Are Not in This Alone* section. Following that, I share one or two financial tips in the *Pursuit of Your Best Self* section that you can start applying on your own journey.

You may feel alone, but I would like to let you know you are not. However, it is up to you to reach out to me, to a bestie, or to a trusted person in your life. There is a light at the end of that tunnel, but you have to do the hard work to get there. I believe you can be your best self! And I am so excited to be a part of your journey towards getting there.

So, let's get started.

CHAPTER 1

The making of me

————•••••○○ ● ○○•••————

Who am I? And how did I become who I am today? Like I explained earlier, I believe the answer to these questions would be based on the result of the combination of genetics, environmental influence, and circumstances. I believe we all have the ability to change to a certain degree, but there's always a point of realization of who we are, why we are the way we are, and who we want to be moving forward. There are several personality traits that pop into my head whenever I analyze myself. And —in my quest for transparency— I will share them with you.

Introvert

Were you born an introvert or extrovert, or did you become one of these two through life experiences? I believe I was born an introvert. Painfully shy and always steering clear of the limelight.

My earliest memory is my first ballet class. I was three –almost four– and my mom was trying to help me overcome my shyness. Yeah, right at the innocent age of three, she enrolled me in my first dance class. Several weeks went by and I would not move off the bench. Not only would I not move off the bench, but I wouldn't let my mother leave.

I kept this up until one day I suddenly got off the bench and joined the rest of the girls on the dance floor. And I "have been dancing ever since." As a matter of fact, in my first recital, I was front and center in the butterfly dance, poised and confident in the lead role as if that was God's sole purpose of creating me on earth.

I would be neglectful if I didn't tell you that my class made the front page of the social section of the Palm Beach Post then.

Yes, yours truly was in the middle of the picture. *Was someone who was born an introvert now on the verge of becoming an extrovert?* Only time would tell.

After performing in that ballet class for the first time, all I ever wanted was to become a dancer. I loved ballet a lot, and jazz was a close second. I vividly remember standing on the dance floor in ballet class, trying my hardest to have perfect posture and precisely pose my feet. To my delight, my ballet teacher noticed me when she walked past... This was a woman I looked up to and admired. I wanted to be able to dance just like her. She asked me what I wanted to become when I grow up. In a proud and serious voice, I said "a ballet dancer." Her response to me was "oh...you do not have the build for a ballet dancer." At age twelve, I was devastated, my dream shattered in an instant. My self-confidence was reduced immediately, and sadness overcame me as I fought back tears.

People Pleaser

This is a tough one to explain. Again, I am not sure if I was born this way, or I gradually developed into one. I tend to think I developed into one. Neither of my parents graduated from college. My mom completed three years but quit and got married. Both my parents worked hard to provide a good home for me and my siblings. My mom was a stay-at-home mom for many years and my dad started and ended his career in the grocery business. As a child, I had no idea how hard my parents worked to ensure we never lacked.

Like most kids and teenagers, there were times when we were not respectful or appreciative of our parents. At the age of ten though, I witnessed some situations my parents had to deal with that made me decide then and there that I was going to try my best to always please them. I did not want to cause them any heartache or grief. I wanted to make them proud. This was the beginning of my quest. Whether it's right or wrong didn't matter, it was always on the back of my mind and the depth of my soul as I navigated through my life. Almost every decision I made henceforth was based on this underlying goal.

Non-confrontational

I definitely think this trait was developed from my introvert nature and innate people pleaser personality. I avoided confrontations at all costs; I rarely spoke up for myself, even when I was supposed to, just for the sake of peace.

During my teenage years, my parents went through a tough time. Financial hardship created tension in the household, and I remember hearing them yell at each other so much that I ended up plugging my ears with my fingers. In case I haven't mentioned, my mom is Italian and wears her emotions on her sleeve. She wasn't the type who kept her feelings or opinions hidden. As a result, it got a bit loud every now and then in our household. I knew right then that I did not want that kind of life for myself.

In Need of a Man

I am not exactly sure how this need came about. From early childhood, I can remember my dad worked long hours. As I mentioned earlier, he was in the grocery store business. When I think about the many events and activities I took part in during my younger years, I recall my mother was always there. But as for my dad, I can probably count on one hand the number of times I remember him showing up.

Was I longing for my dad to be more of an active participant? Did his absence really have that much of an influence on me? In hindsight, I think it did. I wanted a man who would be an active participant in my life. A man who was confident, secure, hardworking, smart, involved, and a decision-maker.

Some of these traits my father possessed and some he lacked. I remember thinking my mother ran the household and my dad was just a silent partner most of the time. And am fairly certain this is one of the reasons I chose the man I chose to marry. I will elaborate on this in the next chapter.

Stubborn streak

In ninth grade, I went to a Catholic high school about a 45-minute drive from our house. I had to ride a bus on a daily basis, so it was hard for me to get involved in extracurricular activities. I decided to switch to a public high school when I got to tenth grade. I knew a few kids from my middle school days at the other Catholic school, but not too many. I was very shy and somewhat of a nerd. I wanted to get involved so I tried out for cheerleading. I had been a cheerleader in middle school, and I had been dancing almost my whole life at that point.

I was fourteen or fifteen, and I vividly remember walking into the high school on the first day of tryouts. As I was walking in, another girl who was new to the school walked alongside me. I remember thinking how pretty and mature looking she was. She was just a year older than I was, but she looked like a woman and I felt like a little girl. Though I kind of felt inferior and intimidated by her, she was very friendly and we hung out together that first day. Later on, I found out she was trying out for Varsity while I had my mind set on JV. And that was a relief; I felt I still had a chance.

Nervous doesn't even come close to describing how I was feeling the night of tryouts. I wanted to back out so badly. It was open tryouts and the gym was full of people I didn't know. We were placed in groups of three. Of course, I was placed with two of the most popular girls from junior high who in my mind had been born with pom-poms in their hands. One was Miss Spirit herself and the other was a superb gymnast. And there was me, Miss Shy and Reserved. I had to do a lot of self-talk to get myself to go through with it. Somehow, I mustered up enough courage to go out there.

Maybe not courage, maybe stubbornness was more like it; I decided I was not going to be a quitter.

During the tryouts, there were things we did individually, and some as a group. The cheer we did together and the jumps were done individually. Both girls blew me away with their spirit and precision during the cheer. The gymnast blew us both away with her jumps. Every time either one of them did something individually, the crowd went wild! When I had to do my jumps alone, I swear to you I could almost hear a pin drop, literally. I think I heard two people clap for me and one was my mother. I wanted to run off that gym floor and just hide, not to mention cry. The last thing I wanted to do was dance. We did this together, and this gave me strength. Then I continued my self-talk, *ok girl, this is your chance.* And bam! I blew them away! I felt so empowered and proud of myself that I stuck with what I was doing, and I didn't give up.

Though I did well on the dance floor, I did not think I made it to the JV squad.

But low and behold, they called my name! Keli Hinchliffe!

Did I hear that right? Why yes, I did! I was chosen to be a JV cheerleader for VBHS!

I was also selected by the coach as one of three captains. I went on and became a Varsity Cheerleader in eleventh and twelfth-grade, too. Not only a cheerleader but a captain as well.

It is amazing how one little success can change the trajectory of one's life. Had I given up or ran off that gym floor, I would not have experienced that feeling of empowerment, accomplishment, and fortitude. Looking back, high school cheerleading was definitely on the list of the top five best experiences of my life. Uncomfortable situations are the best way to grow and find out what you are made of.

Desire to be independent

I remember it like it was yesterday. I was eleven, and my sister got married at a young age. At least, it seemed so then. She was twenty-one and became a mother just after she turned twenty-two. She had her second child shortly after, and as a result, the girls were just shy of two years apart. My sister's marriage did not last. After her second child turned one year old, she got divorced. I was fifteen years old by then.

She started college when she was eighteen but did not finish. She is one of those naturally smart people, but she was not interested in college education. Instead, she worked as a waitress, bartender, and various menial jobs. She was, and still is, a hard worker, and struggled to make ends meet at times. Right after she got divorced, she lived with us in the house I grew up in. My mother and I were the primary babysitters. I loved those girls like they were my little sisters. It still feels like they are my little sisters, not my nieces.

When she finally got a stable job and felt like she could survive on her own and take care of her girls, she moved out of our house. Then they lived in a tiny rental house on a dirt road out west of town. My boyfriend and I assisted her by babysitting my nieces frequently. This was when I realized the depth of my feelings for these girls. I remember thinking that if I were not fifteen, I would have married my boyfriend and adopted those precious girls. I guess my nurturing instincts were kicking in. I actually said this out loud to my mother.

Watching my sister struggle and work hard like she did to make ends meet had a significant impact on my life. I knew at a very young age that I always wanted to be able to take care of myself financially without leaning on somebody else for support. I did not want to have to work as hard as my sister did or rely on anyone for my financial support. Hence, staying in an unhealthy marriage was never going to be an option.

Throughout high school and as a little girl, all I wanted to do was dance. As you already know, my confidence and my dream of achieving that goal were shattered when I was twelve. My new dream was to be a math teacher and the cheerleading coach at my high school. However, the impact of watching my sister's struggles made me decide I needed a more stable and higher-paying career. I enjoyed the accounting class I took in high school. I was quite good at it, I must add. The more I researched the salaries of an accounting career and the stability that comes with it, I realized that was my path, my source of security. Accountants would always be needed in some form or fashion.

Controlled

An introvert who wants to please, who is not confrontational, and is in need of a man is a disaster waiting to happen. Having a strong-willed, tenacious mother and my desire to please other people led to me being self-controlled, but in a self-imposed way. These were choices I made. Granted, I was young and impressionable. But I knowingly made the choice to always make my parents proud. When I say parents, I basically mean my mother because we were closer, and she was more attentive, emotional, vocal, and value-driven.

Hence, she was the one most involved in my life.

Looking back, I feel as if I lived someone else's life; like I was a pawn in someone else's game of chess. Yes, it was self-imposed but it doesn't negate the feelings. Constantly trying to please someone else is exhausting. Now looking back, it feels as if it was an out-of-body experience. Was that really me? What would my life look like today if I had not made the choice to please?

You Are Not in This Alone

#1: Be prepared, not a people-pleaser.

As part of my preparation, and not to mention the source of inspiration for writing this book, I interviewed several women who had gone through divorces. Their professional backgrounds were diverse. Ranging from CPAs, to teachers, politicians, pharmaceutical industry professionals, and MBAs. Some came from wealthy families and others did not. Some had children easily, others had to use medical technology. And some chose not to have any at all.

Regardless of the diversity in their backgrounds and situations, there was a common theme: they either surrendered or gave up their dreams to stay home and raise their children, or they assisted their husbands in pursuing their own dreams and career.

Did you hear me? They gave up their dreams and sometimes careers. It sounds to me like they had the same "people-pleasing" tendency that I had. They all took somewhat of a back seat to support their husbands. So, most of them had to start over with their careers or recreate themselves during or after the divorce. I am not asking you to give up being a stay-at-home mom. I did it and I would make that same decision all over again.

What I am saying is, don't give up on yourself. You don't have to be a people pleaser to make your marriage work. You are just as important as everyone else in your life. Life is about balance. So, take some time for yourself. Keep your skills sharpened. Stay involved with your financial life as well. Know what is coming in and what is going out and where it is going. This can be easier said than done, I am well aware of that. But at least keep this in mind and try to balance so that if that proverbial door closes on your marriage or you find yourself suddenly a widow, you will not be completely stranded.

Pursuit of Your Best Self

Tip #1: Keep your resume up to date.

I am an eternal learner. I'm not even sure if that is a real categorization, but I like the way it sounds. To put it another way, I constantly want to be learning and challenging my mind. Pushing myself to learn and experience things that may seem out of reach or outside my comfort zone. On that same note, I can't stress enough the importance of keeping your resume up to date.

You may be in a healthy, happy marriage, and your current role might be a stay-at-home mom or homemaker. You never know when life is going to throw a curveball at you. It could be a divorce or the death of your spouse. You just don't know. My motto is, "Hope and pray for the best and plan for the worst." That way, you would be better prepared should things change in the future. It is much easier to navigate through tumultuous times if you have balanced your life beforehand than trying to figure it out in the midst of chaos and grief.

Not only should you keep your resume up to date, you should keep your skill set sharp, too. Take some time off for yourself. Take a class centered on something you enjoy or have always wanted to do. It's ok to take some "me time" off. It's okay to be away from your husband, kids, and household responsibilities for some time for yourself. Trust me, everyone would be better off if you do. If you are anything like me, it will rejuvenate you and make you feel like an individual again. Not someone's wife, mom, daughter, etc., but you! My experience has been that if you take time off, your family will appreciate and value you more. I was a better mom both when I was a married and single whenever I took care of myself. Try it, you just might like it.

Tip #2: Make a budget or at least track your living expenses.

One should always know what comes in through the door and what goes out. Whether you're single, married, divorced, or widowed, it doesn't matter. If you don't have control over your money, then your money will have control over you. I do not want to be oblivious to the ins and outs of my money. I want to be in charge. To be able to do that, I needed to make a budget. So do you.

In my experience working with clients as a financial planner, I found most people cringe whenever I say the word *budget*. So, I have found that I get a better response when I say *Monthly Spending Detail*. I know it sounds a bit silly, but it works.

If you are not sure where to begin, then start by tracking your expenses for 3-6 months. Six months is ideal, but three is a good start. I like to separate them into *need-based* and *want-based expenses*. If you aren't sure, just ask yourself, *do I need this to live or is it just something that I want?*

Include everything from house-related expenses, to cars, insurance (home, auto, health, life, long term care, disability, etc.), groceries, entertainment, personal care, pet care, and vacations. Don't forget about camps for the kids (summer and sports), childcare costs, and private schooling. If you are anything like me, you will be amazed at how much you actually spend. This is why so many people are in debt, especially credit card debt.

CHAPTER 2

Why I married the man I married

⸻⸺•••○○ ● ○○•••⸺⸻

*Hindsight is beautiful and eye-opening! I am an analyzer by na-
ture and have analyzed my reasons for marrying the man that I
did. Throughout my teens and twenties, I had some sweet, thoughtful, hardworking, fun, and handsome men in my life. Some that
wanted to marry me. Some that I thought I would marry. Why
didn't I marry one of them? I often cycle back (as I call it) and
try to figure it out. The recurring answer in my mind is, this was
God's will. I have three awesome young men and a wonderful life.
I like who I am today better than who I was many years ago. In
my heart, I know that I would not be who I am today if I had
not chosen the man I chose to marry.*

Engagement

I was living the dream. I had a great job that I loved! Making good
money! Wonderful friends! Living in a fun city! Cheering for an NFL
team! It almost seems surreal looking back. Remember my passion
was and always will be to dance. I actually wanted to be a Rockette
and dance on Broadway. But I was too short, so that dream had to
be altered. I just wanted to dance and perform on stage. I was able
to fulfill that passion and simultaneously have a professional career.
This was better than I had dreamed.

Let's take a step back so you can understand the sequence of
events and what brought me to this utopia in my life. While still
in college, I secured a job with Arthur Andersen as an auditor in
Tampa. At that time, Arthur Andersen was one of the big eight

public accounting firms. These were firms that most accounting graduates aspired to work with.

While I was working with them, a friend of mine convinced me to try out for the Tampa Bay Bucs cheerleaders, better known as the Swashbucklers. I say *convinced* because I had not even thought about dancing for an NFL team, even though I wanted to dance. I didn't think I was sexy enough or had hair that was full enough (in the 80s you had to have the big hair) to be an NFL cheerleader. I was a born introvert and the thought of standing in the front of judges among those other girls trying out scared and intimidated me. Well, she won and I tried out with her. And much to my amazement, I made it! Excited doesn't come close to describing how I felt. Elated, proud, amazed, and somewhat nervous about what I had gotten myself into were just some of my feelings. I cheered with them for two years – one while working at Arthur Andersen and the other while working at my next job as a financial analyst.

I worked at Arthur Anderson for three and a half years before I decided I needed a change. I interviewed with McDonald's Corporation, yes, the Golden Arches, and I got a job as a financial analyst. To say that this was a dream job is an understatement. It didn't start out as a dream job but quickly became one of my favorite and most memorable experiences in my career.

The job itself was a perfect fit for me at this time in my life. It was a job that required professional, academic, interpersonal, and presentation skills. Remember I was and still am an introvert by nature, so presentation skills were difficult for me to conquer. I was forced to take a presentation skills class if I wanted to move up in the company. I was scared to death. My hands would shake and my voice would crack when I had to be videotaped, and then I ended up in sheer embarrassment whenever I watched myself. Looking back, this was a pivotal job. I was put in an uncomfortable position and forced to face one of my fears. Because of that, I became more confident in front of a group of people which helped me grow personally and professionally.

During my tenure with McDonald's, I met a fabulous man. He was handsome, successful, and kind. We had a ton of fun together! We'd dated about a year when he proposed. As a little girl, I always dreamt of this day. I have always envisioned my future husband getting down on one knee, in a beautiful romantic setting and expressing his love for me in a way that would bring tears to my eyes. Well, it was romantic as we were by a lake at night with the moon visible and the sky clear. However, there was no one knee or overwhelming expressions of love. It almost felt more like a business deal. Therefore, there were no tears, just-a-matter-of-fact *yes*.

The Wedding Planning

Let the wedding planning begin! This is what I had been waiting for. I was so excited to start this process: choosing a venue, band or DJ, cake, dress, bridesmaids, food, invitation cards, the engagement party, and bridal and couple's showers. Well, the closer I got to the wedding day, the more reality set in. I felt that something was wrong. Why wasn't I more excited, happier? I felt out of sorts. Praying and soul searching were consuming my days until it finally hit me —I had this wonderful man who loved me but I was doing this for the wrong reasons. I thought this was what I was supposed to do at this point in my life. Most of my friends were married or getting married. Some were even starting to have babies. Was I late to the party? Was I going to end up all alone? These were not reasons to get married.

This was not fair to my fiancée. So I did one of the hardest things I had ever done up to that point in my life; I called it off. I was in tears, and he was heartbroken. I will never forget that moment or those feelings. That was a pivotal moment in my life, surely.

We tried to continue seeing each other but it got to the point where we said "let's be friends." Ultimately it was just too tough on both of us. I needed to get away and have a fresh start. I have always been a believer and prayed, so that is what I did. Five months after I called off the wedding, I was offered a promotion with McDonald's in the Atlanta region. Did I mention that I had everything planned out for the wedding with the exception of sending out invitations and doing my last dress fitting? Yes, we were that close to becoming Mr. & Mrs. He eventually forgave me and, more importantly, I forgave myself. Sidebar —we actually reconnected and are now friends. The move to Atlanta was exactly what I needed at that time.

Met all checklist items

I moved to Atlanta, knowing just one person, and of course a handful of people that I met through working with McDonalds in Clearwater. I wanted to recreate myself: focus on my career, take and pass the CPA exam, and take care of myself. My job in Atlanta was different than in Clearwater. Previously, I worked in the Accounting department and we dealt with the corporate-owned stores. In Atlanta, we dealt primarily with the franchises. There was a learning curve that challenged me professionally but I still loved working for the Golden Arches.

This is exactly what I did the first eighteen months I spent in Atlanta. I focused on learning all I needed to know about my new job and working hard to move up the corporate ladder. I passed my CPA exam and exercised like an obsessed woman. I lived by myself at first but then met some friends through work. I ended up living with one of them. We had lots of fun. I might actually categorize that time of my life as a time when I was a bit of a "party girl".

Although relationship-wise, I failed miserably. I got to a point where I had sworn off guys. I was content with just being alone. I was going to focus on being the best employee, daughter, aunt, sister, and friend I could be. And that was it. At least I tried to convince myself I was content.

I remember this day like it was yesterday. My roommate and another friend of ours from McDonald's were going to a University of Georgia (UGA) game. My roommate begged me to go, but I did not want to. I was not in the mood to party and socialize. Well, my roommate won out. I went, and I actually had fun. We met some guys at the tailgate before the game, then ran into them at a bar afterwards. One of them asked me to dance. I noticed he was an awesome dancer. Of course, that was one of the items on my checklist for a husband. He had to be able to dance. Oh, did I forget to mention I had a checklist? Talk about anal-retentive.

Well, this guy I met at the UGA game checked every box on my checklist. Intelligent, hardworking, took good care of himself, exercised, and ate right (for the most part). He's funny, a good dancer, had a good family, and was a Christian. I was so enamored with him that I thought, *this was the guy I had been waiting for!* There was one thing I did not expect though —he had been married before. No children, but a failed marriage. I must admit it made me stop to re-evaluate whether or not I wanted to continue seeing him. However, I pushed that thought aside and let myself get swept away.

We dated for only short six months when he proposed. Once again, it was not the proposal I had always imagined. We had been at a Braves game and while we were in the car driving back to his place (a high-rise condo in Buckhead), he proposed. He said he had picked up the ring that day and had planned to make it something special, but just couldn't wait. Since he checked all my boxes, and everything seemed right, I said *yes*.

Hang on because this speeds up even more. Since he had been married before and I had called off my wedding two months before the wedding date, neither one of us wanted to have a long engagement. As a matter of fact, we didn't want to wait at all. Thinking back, it was his idea but I just went along with it. Remember I had found the man who checked all my boxes. I didn't want to lose him. Even more prevalent was, I didn't trust myself to follow through with it if I waited too long. I did that once and didn't follow through. Looking back, I didn't want my mother influencing me or my decision either. Remember I was a people pleaser and wanted to make my parents (mom especially) proud. So, we got married about two months after he proposed.

The wedding was a destination wedding, small and intimate; just family and three close friends. I remember standing in the foyer of the little chapel feeling like I was going to faint. My brother asked me "are you sure you want to do this?" My response was *yes*. As I was walking down the aisle, I felt like I was watching someone else's wedding. This was not what I had always dreamed of as a young girl. The self-talk in my head was, "Ok Keli, you agreed to this and there is no stopping it now. You must see this through."

Let's fast forward to the honeymoon, day three to be exact. I had the same self-talk in my head. I remember going into the bathroom because I had tears in my eyes. It wasn't anything he did or said but how he said it to me. That tone of voice I will never forget. I felt like I had never heard him talk to me like that before. It was a condescending tone. That was not on my checklist for sure.

To avoid being controlled

Hindsight is a wonderful thing. I wish I had foresight before making some of the choices I made in my life. I guess if we were omniscient, then we would be God. On second thought, I don't want that job.

One of my biggest hindsight "ah-ha" moments actually happened recently. As I started to write this book and dug deeper into why I am who I am, I realized that some of the most significant relationships in my life were ones where a significant figure in my life was controlling. Yeah, hard to believe, I know. Looking at me now people see a strong, independent woman who is motivated and determined. Sometimes, I want to scream when people refer to or describe me as a strong woman. I know I am, but it's taken a lot for me to get here. And if I may share a moment of vulnerability with you, I'll admit that sometimes, I don't want to be the strong one. I want someone I can count on to be strong when my life takes an unexpected turn or when things get bumpy.

It's hard for me to believe that I ever allowed myself to be in a controlling relationship. If I am honest, then I'll let you know there are really three relationships where I allowed myself to be controlled. Yes, I had a choice and I allowed it. One is with my mother, then my ex-husband, and lastly, a close friend. They all seem so obvious to me now, but that is the beauty of hindsight.

Through many nights of journaling, crying, soul searching, and praying, I came to the conclusion that I rushed into my marriage. I did this for multiple reasons but the prevalent one was that I did not want anyone to influence my decision, especially my mother. I did not want her sharing her thoughts and opinions and eventually swaying my decision. That had happened many times in my life. I feel like she probably did not even realize the influence she had on me.

Thinking back, I believe I met my soul mate in college. We were inseparable. Some people called us two peas in a pod. Everything just worked. We were equally yoked. We were happy! One day, my mother said to me, "you can't marry him because you will have midgets." Yes, she said that. Remember she is my out-spoken, feisty Italian mom. With my first fiancée, she said that he was into name-dropping and appearances. Other boyfriends I had that I really cared about I had always thought, *what will my mother say about him? Would she approve?*

In an effort to avoid my weakness of letting her thoughts and opinions influence my decisions (note I said let), I chose to do a quick engagement. My parents only met my husband once before we got married. And that was totally out of character for me.

Biological Clock

I cannot avoid talking about my biological clock. When I met my future husband, I was 30 years old. I would be lying if I told you my biological clock was not ticking loud and profusely back then. In my mind, if I didn't have babies in my early to mid-30s, then it wasn't going to happen. I'm not sure why it felt that way but, it could be because both my mom and sister were young and in their early 20s when they started having children. Or it could be because my friends were all having children. Regardless, I felt like my time was slipping away.

Remember that my future husband checked all my boxes. Therefore, I assumed we were going to have a long and happy life together with lots of kids. I wanted 4 children: a nice even number that will lead to a houseful of noise, activities, and lots of love; making memories to last for a lifetime. As I have come to realize, what I want does not always coincide with the way life works in a fallen world. God gave me three handsome, intelligent, thoughtful, and hard-working boys, but not the family unit I initially wanted. This is tough to say, even after all these years.

Proving others wrong

I am embarrassed to say this out loud, but I feel compelled to share in an effort to help others. Part of me went through with staying in my marriage for as long as I did to prove others wrong. I have a stubborn streak that has been evident from as early as the age of three. I mentioned my first dance class and how I sat on the bench for weeks with my mother by my side and I wouldn't get up to participate. That was because I didn't want to get up until I was good and ready. Well, that stubborn streak reared its head when I was planning my wedding six weeks before the day of the event. Who does that? Looking back, I felt somewhat like a crazy lady.

The thoughts going through my head were something to the effect that if I don't keep moving and do this now, I won't go through with it. Flashbacks of calling off my big dream wedding kept going through my head and heart. Was it that I had to prove my mother wrong or I had to prove it to myself that I could follow through? I think it was a bit of both and neither of those were the right reasons to get married. Again, there is that hindsight......it's a beautiful thing and it also involves looking in the mirror at your insecurities, fears, and faults.

You Are Not in This Alone

#2: The choice is yours

Wouldn't it be awesome to have a crystal ball and be able to see the consequences of our choices? Even if we did have a crystal ball, would we go back and change things? Maybe, but more likely, we wouldn't. Most of the women I interviewed agreed with me on that. They have become stronger, and more independent as a result of their trials and tribulations.

When I asked them, "why did you marry the man you married?" Some said they were so young when they married their high school sweetheart, they were not mature enough or didn't really have a clue what they were getting themselves into. Others had grown up in dysfunctional families or ones that were struggling financially. They wanted to get out of there and start afresh. Their desire to get out of their current situation somewhat clouded their judgment when it came to choosing husbands. Believe it or not, many of them had similar reasons.

They were born and raised by submissive mothers and had strong, controlling fathers. In their eyes, this was the norm. The man should always be in charge. He should have the career, handle the finances, be taken care of, and made happy. They were made to believe that this was the wife's duty.

The households we grow up in have such an impact on whom we become and the choices we make. However, the keyword is *choices*. We all have choices. Choose to take care of yourself. Choose your reaction to others' behavior. Be in control of who you are. You are the best person to do this. No one can take better care of you than you!

Pursuit of Your Best Self

Tip #3: Request copies of credit reports from 3 credit bureaus (Equifax, Transunion, and Experian).

Do you know that you can get a copy of your credit report from all three credit reporting agencies every 12 months for free? You don't want to request it any more often than 12 months. If you do, it will negatively affect your credit score. I don't request it that often, and I don't recommend doing it that often unless you have a major amount of credit cards or outstanding loans. If you do, then that is something we should definitely address. (*The Balance: How to Rebuild Your Credit after Divorce 6-28-2020*).

When you receive your credit report compare what you have to what is showing on the credit report. If there are any discrepancies, take note of them and do your research. It can be quite time-consuming but well worth it to clean up your credit.

The two most significant things that affect your credit score are the length of time you have had a credit card or loan open, and credit utilization. A good rule of thumb is you want a lengthy credit history so don't close out that card that you have had since college. Another good rule to follow is to keep your credit utilization to 30% or below. I know this requires a little bit of math but you can do it. Credit utilization is the total outstanding balance you have divided by your credit limit (or availability). (Experian: How to Improve Your Credit Score 12-18-2018).

Tip #4: Calculate your worth.

If you are a stay-at-home mom, calculate your worth. Consider all aspects of your job as a stay- at-home mom.

Listen to me and listen closely all you stay-at-home moms, yes you have value! Your job is probably one of the hardest and most important jobs out there. You wear many hats and one of your major responsibilities is to mold and develop your children into becoming productive, responsible, and contributing members of society.

Put a monetary value on your position. I suggest you start with listing all your responsibilities. Just to get your wheels spinning here are a few: teacher, nurse, disciplinarian, activity director, cook, or housekeeper. Think about how much time you spend on each. Quantify it. Research the going rate for those job descriptions. Then back to the math, calculate your salary. What are you worth? Coming from experience you are priceless!

CHAPTER 3

Getting lost

If I had a time machine I would definitely go back and change some of my choices and behaviors in my marriage. I got lost. I allowed it to happen. I was not my authentic self. I thought I was and tried to be who he wanted me to be. I have my reasons for allowing this to happen and I own them. A people pleaser, peacemaker, money, desire to be loved and have a family, these are mine. I'm not proud to admit some of them but this is part of my healing process. I hope and pray my vulnerability and transparency helps you.

Desire to please

As I so vulnerably admitted, I knew my husband was not who I thought he was or, should I say, hoped he was on that third day of our honeymoon. I, being the good Catholic girl, would not even consider divorce. It was just not an option. I was in this for the long haul and I was going to make it work. Notice how I said I was going to make it work? It takes two to make a marriage work and two to get a divorce. This is what a dear friend said to me when I was going through my divorce. The first time she said it, I was angry. I was the victim. I didn't give up on our marriage and leave the family. It took me a few years to realize that what she said was so true. I had to dig deep and figure out what was my part in the demise of our marriage. Then I had to own it.

My desire to please my husband consumed me. I slowly started to lose who I was. I became this other person. A person I didn't even respect. That's a weird place to be but I thought it was the right thing to do at the time. Make him happy. That was my goal above all else. Well at least for the first several years.

One vivid memory was when we had only our two oldest sons. They were sitting at the table in the kitchen: one in a booster seat, the other in a highchair. I was preparing dinner. I was feeding them, keeping an eye on them, and preparing our meal. My husband was sitting at the table impatiently waiting for his meal. I served him his meal and he complained that it was not hot enough. He liked his food hot. My first thought was to say "who the hell do you think you are and why aren't you helping me?" Looking back that's what I should have said. But to keep the peace and to please him, I apologized and continued to take care of my boys. Yes, "my boys." That's how it felt.

Not confrontational

The desire to please, and not being confrontational kind of go hand in hand for me. I think this character trait goes back to my introverted personality that I was born with. This might also have something to do with having such an outspoken, strong-willed mother. I did not like confrontations but really, who does? Maybe some people do, but not me.

I should have confronted my husband and stood up for myself and the boys numerous times throughout my marriage, but I didn't. There were many times I felt like I was doing everything on my own. I wanted a partner, a husband, and an active participant in caring for our babies. I felt like because he was the breadwinner and I was the stay-at-home mom, I had to handle everything. I remember him coming home most days and telling me how exhausted he was from his day....*hint hint*. Not really seeming to care how exhausted I was. As a matter of fact, there were times I would tell him first how tired I was, and then he would immediately tell me how tired he was. I felt like it was a competition, like he was trying to one-up me.

Many times, I felt like whenever he came home from work, he treated me like an employee. Condescending is how I interpreted his words. I felt completely subservient, not an equal at all. Did I let this happen? Thoughts running through my mind were "How dare he"? "I had a great professional career." "What happened to the man I fell in love with, the man who was supposed to be my partner?" I did confront him on occasion when I felt empowered. I was cautious not to upset him because he did have a temper.

The times I confronted him, he was never able to see what I was talking about. And even when he was, he never admitted to being wrong. I actually thought about recording him and playing it back for him so he could hear himself. There were a few times I asked him to go see a counselor with me so we could work through this. His response was, "we are two intelligent people, if we can't figure this out on our own, then we have a bigger problem." Well, true, we did.

Wanted a nice life financially

Yes, I dreamed of having a white picket fence, four kids, two dogs, a loving husband, an awesome dad, and of course money to live a comfortable life. As a kid growing up, I thought we were well off. We lived on the beachside of a small town in Florida. Those who lived on the mainland thought the people who lived on the beach were rich. So, I thought we were.

It wasn't until after I graduated from college that I realized that you had to pay off your credit cards. Like many people, my folks used credit cards as part of their daily routine. When I graduated from college, got a "real" job, and took over my credit card payments, I was in a bit of shock. I hate to admit it, but I had about twelve thousand dollars of credit card debt at this point. I tried to whittle away at it with my big starting salary of twenty-six thousand. In 1988, this seemed like a lot. But looking back, I realized that others in the accounting profession were making way more than I was then. Of course, they had either master's degrees or had passed CPA exams.

By the time I met my future husband, my credit card debt had not gone down but up to seventeen thousand. I honestly thought this was normal. He was good with money and had much better financial habits than I did. I wanted him to teach me so we could get rid of this debt together. Did I fail to mention that he had almost eight thousand dollars of debt himself? So, we set out to get rid of our debt before our one-year anniversary. This was something we both wanted so we worked towards it by focusing on paying down as much as we could each month by not eating out as much and not buying whatever we wanted when we wanted it. We basically put every dollar of disposable income towards paying down our debt. Mission accomplished! We got rid of our debt and I have never carried a credit card balance since.

Wanted to be loved

This is a tough subject to broach for me as I am a bit embarrassed about what I am going to say. I was in the sixth grade when a boy who was older than I am showed an interest in me. I was not even remotely interested at first, and I was painfully shy. Our families were friends. My brother and one of his brothers were best buds for many years so we saw his family frequently.

At my brother's first communion, he was flirting (if you can call it that in sixth grade) with me pretty blatantly. He took pictures of me without me knowing, and even took some right in front of me. I must say it made me a bit uncomfortable. Despite him being so obvious, I started to grow fond of this boy. He was handsome, outgoing, fun and our families were fairly close. Well, that fondness grew into a major crush. When I say major, I mean I thought I loved this boy, up until my sophomore year in college.

Trust me, I had boyfriends between sixth grade and my sophomore year in college, but this boy was always in my heart. The one who got away. I never really understood how someone whom I did not even give a second thought could pursue me and win my heart over at such a young age. And for many years after. It put a shadow over all my relationships during that time. Because he broke my heart, I wasn't going to let anyone else do that again. I put a fortress around my heart and had a hard time letting anyone else in. As you can imagine, I was primarily the one doing the breaking up.

There were a few relationships where the boy or young man broke up with me but that was after college. Those were tough to swallow. Every time it happened, it would set me back a bit emotionally and confidence-wise. Actually, when I met my future husband, I had sworn off men. I had come to terms with the fact that I was going to be alone, and that was okay. Deep down, I really just wanted to be loved, adored, respected, and not hurt again.

Wanted my own family

Growing up with two older sisters, a younger brother, a stay-at-home mom for all of my childhood and most of my brother's childhood, and a hardworking dad was my basis for what a family should be. We didn't always get along, but I like to think we were and still are a close-knit family. Friends and people outside our family always commented on being a bit envious whenever they see us together. We get together often and have lots of fun when we do. Now there are spouses, children, grandchildren, and great-grandchildren in the picture. All in all, there are about twenty-eight of us when the whole family gets together.

Having that type of family created a yearning for me to have a big family of my own. I wanted four kids in total. I wanted to be able to stay home and raise them especially when they were little. I wanted to be a mom! I wanted to create fond memories and fun experiences for my kids. In retrospect, I wanted to be a mom more than I wanted to be a wife. Now I know that this is not the right order. My interpretation of what God intended and that is written in the Bible is that the husband and wife must put each other first above everything else. Besides Him, of course. Well, I did not. We did not put God first either.

I grew up a faithful Catholic: went to church almost every Sunday without fail. I went to a Catholic middle school and started at a Catholic high school but only went there one year before switching to public school. I was the lead usher for the teen Sunday evening service when I was in middle school. I tried to do the right things and be "a good girl."

My husband and I grew up on different ends of the religious spectrum. I was Catholic and he was Baptist. To me, that was like fire and brimstone. In an effort to find some common ground while we were dating, we tried different churches. We tried Methodist, Presbyterian, Church of God, Episcopal, and Non-denominational to name a few. Once we got married, that all stopped. I would ask him to go visit churches with me so we could find a place where we could grow together. He said, "You go find one then let me know which one you like." This is not what I had in mind or what I desired.

It took me a while, but I eventually started visiting churches on my own. Looking back, this was the beginning of the end. Our marriage was no longer two people working as a team, it was the beginning of two individuals living separate lives. Also, by him not wanting to participate in finding us a church home I realized that we had different values.

Have you ever felt like you were watching someone else's story and you could see that things were going astray? You wanted to help but you couldn't? Like talking to the TV and trying to steer the characters away from the wrong direction. Slowly, you could see them heading down the wrong path and that things were unraveling. It was a feeling that seemed out-of-body. This wasn't me. This wasn't my life, my marriage. How did I get here? I wanted to stop but I couldn't. The Catholic girl in me said, "Divorce is not an option, you need to make it work. Be the best mom you can be." Because it felt like I was failing miserably as a wife.

You Are Not in This Alone

#3: Explore the why

Getting lost can be easy to do especially when you are young and in love or older and in love for that matter. I feel as human beings, especially women, we want to be loved and in love. I feel like that desire can be so strong, and more so at certain times in our lives. For example, I feel like my biological clock was ticking and that was a part of my why. Why did I rush things, why didn't I take my time to get to know him, why did I tolerate a relationship that was not everything I wanted or at least most of what I wanted?

I asked the women I interviewed the same questions. The most common response was "I was too trusting." Looking back, they could easily identify moments in time when they just trusted their spouse. Even though the tiny voice inside them was saying, "Something is not quite right" or "something is wrong, pay more attention." Why do we ignore the red flags? Are we so afraid of being alone that we are okay with overlooking the obvious? Why do we let ourselves get lost?

Complacency was another popular response. Many said they were so focused on raising their children and being homemakers that they didn't want to pay attention, or they had little energy left at the end of the day. They had defined their roles in the marriage and there was no deviation. In hindsight, they all wished they had known what was going on and what they had financially. Not being more involved with their finances was a common regret. I feel like this is so important for women even if they have a happy, healthy, loving relationship. I can attest to the fact that life doesn't always turn out the way we planned. Not one woman knows when she may be suddenly single due to divorce or the death of a spouse.

Another popular response was, "I was not allowed." This one is hard for me to wrap my head around. I am and always have been a strong-willed individual. I think I got this trait from my mother. She has many stories about me that she would love to share with you, I'm sure. So, to not be allowed to know about your financial life, what you have and where you have it, actually gets me fired up. This was mentioned by more than one of my interviewees. My thought is, this stems from their upbringing. I dated a guy in college whose mother had never driven a car. His father didn't want her to. Knowing this family well, I believe it was because he was old-fashioned as well as concerned about her safety. However, this is not always the case. Some men do things like this as a means to control.

Some men don't allow their wives to be involved with their financial life because they take the Bible too literally and take verses out of context. Several verses talk about a woman submitting to her husband or how she is weaker. 1 Timothy chapter 2:11-12 says "Let a woman learn quietly with all submissiveness. I do not permit a woman to teach or to exercise authority over a man: rather, she is to remain quiet." In these verses Paul is speaking in the context of worship in the church, he is not saying that a wife is always supposed to remain quiet. Also, 1 Peter 3:7 says, "Likewise husbands, live with your wives in an understanding way, showing honor to the woman as the weaker vessel, since they are heirs with you of the grace of life, so that your prayers may not be hindered." Even though some people will use this to say that women are weaker, reading the entire verse demonstrates that is not the sole focus of the verse. The point is that women are to be shown honor and are valued because they are created in the image of God just like men. I am a bit old-fashioned and believe that a man should open doors for a woman, walk on the sidewalk closest to the street to protect her and, all in all, be chivalrous. However, this should be done out of respect and adoration and not as a control mechanism. Likewise, a woman should respect and adore her husband. However, like I tell my boys, these things are earned by the way you treat others and others treat you.

Pursuit of Your Best Self

Tip #5: Know what you have.

Stay involved with finances even if one person is more knowledgeable than the other. At a minimum at least know what you have.

Knowledge is power and has an important part in you knowing who you are and where you are going. I cannot stress this enough. If you are in the happiest, healthiest utopia of a marriage, please, please, please be involved with, or at a minimum, know what you have financially as a couple. It amazes and actually saddens me that there are many women out there who neither have a clue about their marital finances nor do they care to know.

Like I mentioned earlier, even if you are in the best of a marriages, you just never know what life has in store for you. One day, you might wake up and find yourself all alone either through the sudden death of your husband or divorce. I am well aware of the fact that not everyone works with the same side of their brain. That's what makes the world go round.

If you are a right-side brain all the way, this may be way out of your comfort zone. These are people who are more creative and artistic. My best advice is to find yourself a financial planner whom you could trust. One that will educate, not mishandle your stuff. Someone that will keep you in the loop as to what you have, what is being done with it, and why. I think I know that perfect person...me!

Tip #6: Freeze any joint accounts you fear your spouse will try to tamper with.

This is a delicate matter. There may be a phase in your divorce where you haven't really made the decision yet to divorce each other, and you are in sort of a limbo. I would only suggest this when you are ready to move forward with the divorce. Just keep in mind that if you freeze joint accounts, then they'd be frozen for both of you. No movement in or out.

I personally did not have to do this with my divorce. It was amicable and he was more than willing to work with me when it came to financial matters. I would be an advocate of freezing joint accounts if you suspect that your spouse will try to deplete what you have in them. We don't want to believe that the person we loved so dearly at one point would do that but it can happen.

From my past experience with walking with clients as well as friends through the unpleasant and sometimes awfulness of divorce, people scorned will do things you might never have imagined. Back to my motto "Hope and pray for the best and prepare for the worst." (The Ascent: Getting Divorced? Here's What Happens to Your Joint Accounts 10-3-2020).

CHAPTER 4

Making it work

My reasons for trying so hard to make my marriage work and the reasons of other women out there who have been through similar situations may not all be the same. One common thread is that we were motivated to fight for and make our marriages work. My reasons were my faith, stubbornness, determination, desire for a family, and fear of not having money. Some of these reasons were positive, and some not so much. The women I interviewed had similar reasons for fighting for their marriages: because of the children, because of their fear of not having money, and more interesting to me is that they felt like they had a responsibility to take care of their man almost in a caretaking way. Not that I didn't have this desire. But for me, I always thought of marriage as a partnership and not one having more caretaking responsibility than the other. I still feel this way.

Catholic Upbringing

For as long as I can remember, church has been an integral part of my life. As a child, my mother made sure my brother and I went to church every Sunday unless we were sick or out of town. Even when we traveled as a family, which was primarily for summer vacation, she would try to find a church wherever we were. My dad did not go with us on a regular basis, but he usually attended with us on holidays and special occasions.

My mother was and still is a devout Catholic, and that's how I was brought up. For a period of time, I actually went to a catholic school. We moved to the town where I grew up when I was in first grade.

At that time, my mother tried to get me admission into the catholic school which went from first to eighth grade. When we moved there was not an opening in the catholic school, so I went to the public elementary school. It wasn't until fifth grade that there was an opening in the catholic school, so my mom grabbed it and off I went in my jumper and tube socks (it was the mid to late seventies after all).

I loved my catholic school. And to this day, my closest friends were from the friendships I made in fifth through eighth grade. We still do girls' trips together, chat on the phone, pray for each other and our families, and support each other when one of us is going through a tough time. It's not just girls, some of the guys are part of our close-knit group, too. Truly, I feel blessed to have these beautiful people in my life.

As it relates to my marriage, I kept hearing my inside voice say, "divorce is not an option; you need to make this work." As a result of having been born and bred in Catholic doctrine, that's what I have always thought. My close Catholic friends were all still married, and as a matter of fact, still are. They are in it for the long haul, so I thought I needed to do the same. Also, my parents at the time I got married had been married for forty-four years. Fast forward to today and they will be celebrating their sixty-eighth wedding anniversary in 2021. I'm so proud of them for enduring the hardships, persevering, and not giving up. I wanted that kind of love, commitment, and respect. I still do.

Stubborn

Some might say that the underlying reason I tried to make my marriage work was my Catholic upbringing. But I often wonder if it isn't more attributable to my stubbornness. There are multiple examples of my stubborn streak going as far back as Uncle Dicks. This was a two to three year program my mother enrolled me in with the urging of her best friend and neighbor. My mother said she was peeking through the window to see how I was adjusting and I was not doing so well. I was in a rocking chair in the corner of the room, crying. My mother couldn't stand it, she went in and pulled me out of the program. Knowing myself like I do now, I'm pretty sure

I resorted to crying in there because I did not want to do what the teacher wanted me to do.

More examples are my first ballet class, which I already shared with you, trying out for the public high school cheerleading squad while hardly knowing anyone, calling off my first wedding only eight weeks before the wedding day, I could go on and on. Yes, I have a stubborn streak or, some might call it determination. I'm not sure where it came from actually; neither of my parents were overly stubborn. Although I can tell you for sure that I passed it on to one of my boys… lucky me. Or should I say lucky him?

When it came to my marriage, I dug my heels in and was going to make it work. Notice the "I" was going to make it work. Well, let me tell you this, like I mentioned before, it takes two to make it work and two to make it fail. Since marriage is two people working as a team, if all participants are not striving for the same goal, it may end up in the demise of the marriage. As hard as I worked and as much as I wanted my marriage to work, I could not do it alone. I came to that realization fairly early on in the marriage but resigned to the fact that this was how it was going to be. This was my life. This was the hand I was dealt as my oldest sister likes to say. This is the path I chose, outside of God's will I might add, because I hadn't been listening to God's promptings. Therefore, this was my destiny. No options. Talk about stubbornness.

My desire to have children was a strong urge inside me, like a gravitational pull. I remember thinking, *I can make this work so I can have my children, the ones I so desired.* Looking back, I feel a bit selfish. I was thinking about me, only me. Why didn't I think about my children to come? Why didn't I play things out in my head and guess that things weren't going to work as I planned; that he would leave? I feel as if I did my children a disservice. Like I let them down. My heart aches when I think about how they have been affected by the divorce.

I would go through every mistake, heartache, grief, loneliness, and angry feeling all over again to get to where I am today. Never in a million years would I change a thing. The only thing I would change is how my children were affected. Taking a step back though, this is part of me becoming who I am. But the children were definitely impacted for good or bad. God used this to make me into the person

He wanted me to be and to make my boys into the men He wants them to become. Have I mentioned how blessed I feel to have three handsome, intelligent, motivated, and determined young men? They are my pride, my joy, and my heart! God also blessed me with the ability to start my own business. He blessed me with an awesome support group. Most importantly, He blessed me with a relationship with Him.

Not a quitter

Stubbornness and not being a quitter go somewhat hand in hand in my book. Stubbornness to me is more obstinate and almost has a negative connotation. Whereas not being a quitter has a more positive meaning. To me, it means pushing through uncomfortable situations, stepping outside your comfort zone, and believing you can achieve your dreams. Yes, I was both.

My stubbornness seemed to get me in trouble or in situations that caused me heartache and grief. My "not a quitter" attitude led me to the accomplishment of many of my dreams. Some that I didn't even know I had until they happened. One such dream was being an NFL cheerleader. I had always wanted to be a professional dancer and specifically dance on Broadway. But my introvert nature kept me from pursuing this dream. Much to my amazement though, God had a different plan for me. He used a dear friend of mine to convince me to try out for an NFL cheerleading team. This was not even on my radar. However, my friend begged me, so I decided to give it a shot. I was extremely surprised that I made it. In that situation, not being a quitter paid off.

As for my marriage, not being a quitter did not turn out the same way. As I've said before, it takes two to make a marriage work and two to make it fail. I was trying hard to make it work. Well, at least in the first five years. There came a point when I chose not to love him anymore. You heard me; I chose. I chose to just co-exist with him and focus all my energy and attention on our boys. When I think back now to that last year we were together, I was pushing him away. I did not like him because of the way he spoke to me, his desire for me to get a nanny so we could go and do activities outside the house, and the fact that he "did not want to sit at home to eat popcorn and watch TV on a Friday nights." I couldn't believe he actually said that to me. Was I quitting? Was I just changing my focus to be the best mother I could to our boys? I knew in my heart I was miserable and there was no way I could raise our boys in that type of environment.

Desire for a family

My boys are everything to me. I'm not sure of the bible verse but I know the bible alludes to the fact that marital relationship must come first. By doing that, the children learn what a husband and wife relationship should be; what God intended. I feel the stronger the marital relationship, the stronger the family unit.

Well, I forgot about that or I gave up. I'm not really sure which. I do know my desire to have a family was overwhelming to me at times, almost in a selfish way. I wanted a happy, healthy marriage and four kids. Oh, don't forget two dogs. Was I wearing rose-colored glasses? Was I so focused on that dream that I could not see things that were right in front of me? There were signs. Signs that I was not paying attention to or perhaps, I didn't want to see.

Money

Money has always been a motivating force for me. From seeing my sister struggle as a single mom to my parents using credit cards to make ends meet, I knew from a young age that I did not want money to dictate my life choices. I did not want it to control me.

When my ex-husband and I got married, we were making the same amount of money. We were both hard workers and committed to paying off our debt by the end of our first year together. We accomplished that. My plan after the birth of our first child was to go back to work, at least part-time. However, my husband started making better money with the potential for sizable growth. So, we made the decision for me to be a stay-at-home mom. The best decision I made, but the hardest job I've ever had.

When my marriage seemed to be unraveling and changing for the worse, the thought of putting my babies in daycare made me sad. There was no way. I wanted to be there every day, now more than ever. To witness all their stages of development, to take them to the playground, to read them stories, and rock them to sleep. I think I was afraid of not being able to do that. Not having the money to allow me to do that. This was definitely a driving force in my eagerness, stubbornness, or whatever you want to call it to make my marriage work.

This is hard to admit and makes me extremely vulnerable, but I remember standing in front of my bedroom mirror when things were really getting tough and saying to myself, "Well, as long as he allows me to stay home and buys us the things we need, I can tolerate this unhealthy marriage." I am ashamed to admit that now. Where was I? Who was I? Was God disappointed in me? Where were my values?

You Are Not in This Alone

#4: Why women tried to make it work

There can be many reasons behind your motivation for making it work. It could be your religious upbringing, your personality, or your desires. Mine was a combination of all three. It was my catholic upbringing, my stubbornness, and my desire to have a family that led me to continue to try to make my marriage work. Like I've mentioned before, it takes two to make a marriage work, and believe it or not, it takes two to make a marriage fail.

The women I interviewed had motivations similar to mine for trying to make their marriage work. Some of these they were blatantly aware of, and others became obvious to them either during or after their divorce. One of the most popular reasons was "for the children." All of the women I spoke with had an indescribable love for their children. They would do anything to take care of them, make them happy, and protect them. Along with this intense love is a pang of overwhelming guilt when your marriage is failing and you are thinking about breaking up the family unit. One of the women told me that she stayed way longer than she should have because of this guilt. Her situation actually had to get to the point of physical abuse before she took that step of filing for a divorce. Ultimately, it got to a point when it was no longer safe for her or her children.

Another reason for staying too long in a marriage that is obviously not working is money. Almost all the women I spoke with had given up their careers in one way or another to stay at home with the children. They had been out of the workforce for quite some time. This is a scary thought when you are not sure if you will be able to support yourself not to mention your children. It's hard to believe, but sometimes, child support is not much at all. It really depends on the judge, your attorney, and how amicable you are with your spouse or soon-to-be ex-spouse. This is one of the reasons I mentioned in the first chapter, Making of Me, that we women should always keep our skills sharpened and ourselves marketable from a career standpoint.

Many women tend to be nurturers and caretakers by nature. This was also a common response from the women I interviewed. They felt like they had to take care of their spouse. It was their job. Maybe they decided this on their own, maybe it was an agreement that they had before going into the marriage, or maybe they just evolved into this caretaking mode. Regardless, I feel like this is dangerous territory. I reluctantly admit that I fell into this caretaking mode. It was of my own doing. I felt that he was working and taking care of us financially, so my job was not only to take care of the children and the home but him. Mine got to the point where I let him do basically whatever he wanted. I accepted behaviors that I would never in a million years accept from anyone now or in my past. I'm not sure how I got to this place, but I can tell you I did not like or recognize myself.

However, I take full responsibility for my behavior. If I could rewind the clock and do things all over, I would not have fallen into this mode. In my heart, I feel that not only did I lose respect for myself, but he lost respect for me as well. This could have been the beginning of the end.

Pursuit of Your Best Self

Tip #7: Think about the long-term consequences.

Think about the long-term consequences of the assets you ask for. They might have tax implications.

First, it's important for us to know what marital property is. In a nutshell, marital property is all income and assets acquired by *either* spouse during the marriage. This includes but is not limited to 401(k)s and other employer retirement plans along with Traditional IRAs and ROTH IRAs. It also includes property that you might not necessarily think about, such as deferred compensation, stock options, restricted stocks and commissions, country club memberships, annuities, life insurance, brokerage and bank accounts, real estate, cars, boats, art, antiques, and tax refunds. (Garofalo Law Group: The Long Term Asset Issue 5-27-2020).

Many times, the tax implications of the marital property being divided are often overlooked. I cannot stress enough the importance of considering the tax implications before you go to the proverbial negotiating table. Below are some important points and examples:

- Property transfer incident to divorce from one spouse to the other generally will not result in taxable gain or loss. However, divorcing couples should be made aware of requirements in the IRS Code that make a transfer considered as incident to divorce.
- Alimony prior to 12-31-2018 was taxable to the recipient and tax-deductible by the payor. For divorcees finalized starting 1-1-2019 through 12-31-2025, alimony is not taxable to the recipient and therefore not deductible by the payor. We can thank the Tax Cuts and Jobs Act (TCJA) for this change.

However, this change may only be temporary. The TCJA is set to expire on 12-31-2025. So only time will tell the fate of alimony payments and their taxability.

Be extra careful when it gets to the portion of your spouse's employer retirement plan. This is a tax-deferred asset. What this means is that no tax has been paid on this money. Therefore, when money is disbursed or withdrawn, that tax will be owed. The tax owed could be Federal or State (depending on which state you live in) and potentially an Early Withdraw Penalty of 10% (this comes into play if you are under 59 ½).

For example, in my state, Georgia, if you were to get a portion of your spouse's 401k plan and you took it in cash, then you would owe Federal tax (let's estimate 22%), Georgia state tax of 6%, and an Early Withdraw Penalty of 10% for a total of 38% being paid in taxes. RED ALERT. To avoid all these taxes and penalties, you must have a QDRO in place at the time your divorce papers are signed. What is a QDRO? It's a Qualified Domestic Relations Order which basically states that you are to receive whatever portion agreed upon in the same manner it is currently held (i.e., tax- deferred). This will require you to open a Traditional IRA and move the money over as a custodial transfer. What this means is that the check is not made out to you. It is made out to the custodian (or the brokerage firm, bank, etc.) that is going to hold your IRA for you.

This is huge. It's necessary to prevent a sizeable amount of your asset going straight to Uncle Sam.

Investment accounts often get overlooked as well. I always explain the taxation of investment accounts to my clients as the bucket of your assets that you are "keeping up with the taxes on an annual basis." What I mean by this is, investment accounts may have many holdings in them (e.g., stocks, mutual funds, exchange-traded funds). The holdings more than likely were not all purchased at the same time; thus they have different origination dates. If the holdings are held for less than 12 months and then sold, this will produce a short–term capital gain. Short-term capital gains are taxed as ordinary income rates which are typically higher than the capital gains rate. If the holdings are held for longer than 12 months, then it is a long-term capital gain and thus taxed at a lower rate typically. This could have a considerable impact on the taxes that you owe. Also, not all of the holdings are equal as to the interest and dividends they produce. Some of the holdings may have higher dividends and interest than others. My point is, don't think because you are splitting something evenly that the future tax implications are even too. They may not be. Therefore, do some digging, or better yet, hire an experienced financial planner with a CPA background to help you out. I just may know someone that fits that description...it's me again! (Journal of Accountancy: Tax Considerations When Dividing Property in Divorce 4-1-2013).

Pursuit of Your Best Self

Tip #8: Consider the right to claim children as dependents on your tax return.

This is not an easy subject to broach. In no way do I intend to talk about the children like they are negotiation tools or bargaining chips. Well, let me say this loud and clear...THEY ARE NOT! Like I explained previously, I am a staunch advocate of keeping the children first and foremost. When I was going through my divorce and even to this day, I thought about how every decision I make will affect my boys, and of what impact it will have on them now and in the long haul.

Nonetheless, when it comes to your finances and tax implications, the ability to claim the children as dependents needs to be considered. Typically, the parent with whom the children spend the most time may claim them as dependents. If the children spend equal time between both parents, then the parent with the highest adjusted gross income may claim the dependents.

Sometimes in divorce settlements, the noncustodial parent may ask for the right to claim the children as dependents. If the custodial parent agrees, they may release a claim to exemption for the children. This allows the noncustodial parent to claim the children as dependents and claim the child tax credit for the children if the requirements are met. (E-File: Divorced or Separated and Income Taxes 11-13- 2020).

CHAPTER 5

Summer from hell

This was the hardest chapter for me to write because it stirs up lots of painful memories and feelings. But I had to get it out. I wanted to share with you my confusion and pain. As much I would like to, I cannot take this away from you, no one can. But I can let you know that you are not alone. Others like me have gone through this before you. You are not alone unless you choose to be.

Confused

I remember it like it was yesterday. I am not proud to say that, but it just shows you how traumatic it was for me. Typically, the events in my life that I remember most vividly are those that seem to be on the extremes. Those that make me burst with joy and happiness and those that sadden me and cause me grief. My summer from hell was one of the latter, one of overwhelming sadness and grief.

It was the summer of 2003. Actually, it started in February 2003 when my husband suddenly did a one-hundred-and-eighty-degree turn. I often would describe it as someone turning the light switch off. He had been a model father and husband since the birth of our 3rd child. Suddenly, about three months after the birth, he was a completely different person, hence, the light switch analogy. And bam! Just like that, it felt to me like he checked out on us.

It started with a night here or a night there where he would either stay out really late or not come home at all. Here I am with 3 small children all under the age of 5, and one of them an infant. As anyone who has had children knows, you don't get much sleep with an infant. My lack of sleep was compounded with even less sleep as I would wake up in the middle of the night wondering where my husband was. I would not wish this on anyone.

Being the protective mother that I was, I tried not to let my children know or be impacted by this change in our home. I got the youngest one off to K4, school for 4-year-olds like preschool, and the other two I kept involved in their playgroups and music class. Inside, I was in turmoil. It felt like there was a tornado in me that was slowly gaining strength. Like I was going to shatter and fall apart, and it kept getting worse.

I remember trying to talk with my husband. I even read the Five Love Languages book so I could understand his love language as well as mine. I asked him to sit down with me so I could share my thoughts and findings from this book. He said no, that he wasn't interested in that kind of stuff. I felt like he was so closed off almost like he had this wall built that could not be penetrated. I felt like he did not want to face our problems much less solve them. Here comes my transparency and vulnerability, I had a part in this slow breakdown of our marriage. Yes, I did.

Like I mentioned before, it takes two to have a happy, healthy marriage and two to have it fall apart. The main difference is that I was willing and wanted to seek outside help. I wanted to save our family. I wasn't sure if it was possible at that point, but I wanted to give it my best shot.

Lost

I would say around May 2003 was when I started to hit the lowest of lows. I could not even force a smile on my face. I was so sad. Looking back on my life, this was the most horrible place that I had ever been and I do not care to go there again. I had to give him an ultimatum for my sake and primarily the sake of the children. My ultimatum was that we either go to couples counseling or I would have to make a difficult decision. Our home and family life were not healthy. I was not healthy. I told him I could not continue to live like this. He agreed to couples counseling but looking back, it was too late. At this point, unbeknownst to me, he was already having an affair. The counselor was not engaging at all. He really just sat there and listened and didn't make any comments or suggestions. No homework assignments, not that we would have gotten them done anyway. Alone does not even describe how I was feeling. I felt like this was not my life and I was going through the motions with numbness in my body. Empty and lifeless are other feelings I had. I'm sure my children had to notice even as little as they were. Sometimes I hate myself for that. I felt like I failed them.

As the summer of 2003 progressed, things were getting worse by the day. His one or two nights away from home turned into four or five. I questioned him and the response was always, "I am staying at my buddy's house because I can't stay here." I remember him saying that every time he came back home his stomach would get in knots and he just couldn't relax. Silly me...I believed him. In hindsight, I am sure his stomach hurt and was in knots. But why? At this point, I could only speculate. But to be honest with you, I did not think it was because of infidelity. The only thing that was obvious to me was that I could not control or change his behavior. The only person I could control was myself.

In an effort to find my happiness again, I planned a girls' trip with some of my best friends. We went to the beach for a long weekend. I was sad, stressed, and totally out of sorts. But I went anyway. I tried to find some happiness and laughter, I call this my sunshine, but it was not working. One of my friends was taking classes to become a massage therapist. She noticed that my shoulders were shrugged almost in a permanent position. Also, she noticed the stiffness in my neck due to the stress. At this point, I could barely turn my head to either side because I was so stiff. She attempted to massage me but it was painful, to say the least.

The next day, we were off to the beach. The beach has always been my happy place and where I felt closest to God. We spent maybe an hour on the beach then we went to grab some lunch.

During lunch, I had to excuse myself from the table as I was not feeling well. I went to the ladies' room thinking I was going to be sick. I wasn't sick at all. In hindsight, I think I was having an anxiety attack or a nervous breakdown. I had never experienced one of these before, so I was not really sure. I do remember that I ended up sitting on the bathroom floor.

For those of you who don't know, I am a bit of a germophobe. I have relaxed as I have gotten older, but back then, I really was germophobic. My friend who massaged me the night before came to check on me and saw me on the floor. She sat down with me and just hugged me. Well, the tears just poured out of me. I needed that more than I knew.

I had always been a happy, positive person; one that carried her own sunshine with her, regardless of the circumstances. My mom used to call me sunshine. Even to this day, she still calls me that. During the summer of 2003, I lost that girl. I lost that positive attitude and happy disposition. I felt robbed of that. I felt like my children were robbed of that, too. I can't get that time back —it's been lost forever and brings tears to my eyes when I think about it.

Blindsided

The summer progressed and slowly rolled into the fall. Looking back, I was depressed, confused, and lost. I did not know where to turn or who to confide in. I felt alone, so alone. I'm not sure how I mustered up the energy or even came to think of what to do. It must have been God and my desperate cries for Him to take over.

I remember one night so vividly that when I close my eyes, I can relive it. I was not sleeping well, which was unusual for me, and I was crying myself to sleep most nights. Well, one night, I was crying and I completely surrendered to God. I wasn't even sure of what and how to do this. So I just closed my eyes and said, "God I can't do this anymore. I give up. Help me." I fell asleep and about 30 minutes later, I woke up to God's voice speaking to me. It was so real that I felt like He was right there in my bedroom with me. I sat up and looked around, thinking someone had gotten into my house. But no one was there or at least no physical being. I knew the voice I heard was God's. I knew He was there with me. He said to me, "You are the shining star of this family and I am with you." I laid back down and slept like a baby for the rest of the night. I needed it desperately. I needed Him desperately.

The very next day, I had the idea of hiring a private investigator. I had been digging around trying to figure out what was going on by myself, but I was not having much success. A dear friend of mine suggested a PI and she had the perfect one in mind. I called him and interviewed him. I did everything he advised and answered his questions. He was going to start mid-week.

Well, on Monday night, we had our last counseling session. At the time I did not realize it was our last until we walked out of the office. My husband walked me to my car. I was sitting in the driver's seat with my door open and he was standing right there next to me. I said to him, "I am going to ask you one more time," because I had asked him this question two other times during my summer from hell. I asked him, "Have you or are you cheating on me"? He looked down at the ground and nodded his head *yes*.

He could not look at me or speak the words. Then he tried to hug me. Oh no, I said emphatically, do not touch me! I was blindsided for sure. I did not expect that he would ever cheat on me. I really thought he had more respect for me than that. In fact, throughout the early years of our marriage, I had asked him to make me a promise. The promise was, if he ever had the temptation or thought about having an extramarital affair, that he would give me the courtesy and respect to have a conversation with me first. Not only was I blindsided but so were our close friends.

In all honesty, I was blindsided, yes, but a huge wave of relief came over me. I had been carrying this weight, this burden of not knowing why my marriage was falling apart. Now I knew. I could breathe again and it felt like a huge weight had been lifted off my shoulders. Needless to say, I did not need the PI. Not anymore.

Revelation

The revelation that he had been lying to me and that there was someone else cut me to the core. At least for the most part, I knew what I was dealing with. Now it was time to pull myself together and take care of my boys. I like to say that it was time to put my big girl panties on and take charge. That's exactly what I did. I methodically came up with a sort of to-do list. This is one of my strongest traits; the ability to compartmentalize and put on whatever proverbial "hat" is necessary at different points in my life.

The first item on the list was: to figure out who it was and to confront her. Don't get me wrong, it was mine and my husband's fault first and foremost. However, she had a role in the demise as well. I didn't want to yell or scream, I just wanted her to see that it was not just a woman she hurt but it was three small, handsome little boys. It was a family. They were so sweet and innocent. This is what breaks my heart even to this day. And I am not sure if I will ever feel any differently about that.

I didn't waste much time. The day after I found out about the infidelity, I found out who she was and where she worked. I had my sources —my support system. It happened that she worked for the same company he did. I got dressed and looked classy and sophisticated, I must say. I dropped my oldest off at K4 while the two younger ones and I went to her place of work. I could tell when I walked in, that the other employees knew who I was. I asked to speak with her.

When she walked into the foyer area, I said, "Hi, I am Keli Hazel." I proceeded to introduce my two boys and mentioned that I had just dropped my oldest off at school. She asked if I wanted to go into her office to talk. I said no, and I turned and walked out just as calmly as I had walked in. Wow, that felt good! Empowering! I was not going to be a victim. I was going to hold my head high and deal with the hand I was dealt with, with the utmost dignity and class.

I always want to be able to look my boys, now turned young men, in the eyes and let them know I did my best to fight for and keep our family together. I have no regrets on how I handled or continue to handle the divorce and its aftermath. I just wanted to take care of my boys.

You Are Not in This Alone

#5: You can only control how you respond

Over a year ago, I had a client come in for an initial consultation. She was referred to me by a colleague. Side note...I am proud to say that I get 99% of my clients through referrals. I am truly blessed to have such a great group of clients! This prospective client was still grieving the loss of her marriage and was completely blindsided by what and how it happened. I am not going into details as to protect the innocent. Well, having gone through a divorce myself, I could feel her grief, sadness, confusion, and loneliness.

She had neither handled their finances nor had a good handle on what they had. When I have clients like this, whether through divorce or the death of a loved one, it's hard for me not to cry when they cry. Typically, my eyes get a little watery. Well, I held it together and told her we would take this one step at a time. I would walk with her during this difficult time and educate her on what she had and what I was recommending and why. She would be involved every step of the way.

I was fortunate enough to have a good friend refer me to a divorce financial analyst Krys, at the time I was going through my divorce. She became a friend and professional resource to me. She eventually became my financial advisor while I was still a stay-at-home mom. Now that I am a financial planner with a passion for helping women, I want my clients and prospects to know and feel that they have someone on their side. Especially those that have become suddenly single and are confused, feeling lost, and alone. I want them to know I am here to help them.

Today, my client is thriving and feels more secure and aware of her financial life than ever. For those who have gone through divorces or may in the future, the pain, sadness, and grief rarely leave you completely. At some moments in time, I can still feel all those feelings when I think of a time during my divorce and even post-divorce. They are not there often but I can easily recall how I felt when I put myself back there. On a positive note, those negative feelings do lessen and start to fade the more time goes by. My analogy for this is like having an ax or sledgehammer: the divorce, especially if you did not want it or expect it is the ax or sledgehammer. Imagine that you take that ax or sledgehammer and swing it into the ground. The painful parting, the blade is buried deep and gone but the handle still sticks up slightly from the ground. Sometimes it is more visible or pronounced. And other times, you can barely see it. To me, that exemplifies the memories.

I have learned to accept my divorce and believe there is a reason for everything. I may not like the fact that I got divorced and I definitely do not like that my children had to go through it and grow up without seeing a loving, healthy husband and wife relationship. As a wise man once shared with me, I can only control my own behavior, I cannot control others. However, I can control how I respond to other people's behavior. That is key to living your best life and being your best self! That is what I try to instill into every divorcee that comes to me. Not only does it work for divorcees, but it also works for widows. As a matter of fact, it applies to everyone if you really think about it.

Pursuit of Your Best Self

Tip #9: Open a separate account at a different bank. Start putting extra cash in there for a rainy day. Stash some cash in a safe place.

If you are contemplating a divorce or feel like your spouse may be feeling the same and wonder whether you should open your own separate bank account, the right advice is: _maintain the status quo until the divorce is finalized_. I say the right advice because there are always exceptions to the rule. If both you and your spouse's earnings have always been deposited in a joint bank account, there is probably no reason for you to open up a separate bank account until the divorce is finalized. The logistics of who pays what bills is another pivotal decision that could lead to establishing separate bank accounts.

We know that life is unpredictable and there is no cookie-cutter answer for everyone. There can be unique situations and exceptions to the rule. One such exception is if your earnings are the only source of income deposited in the joint account and your spouse is either unemployed or underemployed and has been "squandering" or removing the funds from the joint account without a mutual agreement. Then for sure, I would open up a separate bank account. (Atlanta Divorce Law Group: Should I Open a Separate Bank Account If I Am Ready To File For Divorce? 2021).

Another exception, well at least it was in my own situation, was I had been a stay-at-home mom for 5 plus years. I had no source of income on my own. My earnings capacity was there but I had no regular job at the time of my summer from hell. Therefore, I stashed away ten bucks here and twenty there when I could and put it in a safe place. My intention was this would be money I would use to secure an attorney if it came down to divorce. In my heart, I wanted to believe that my husband would do the right thing but, in my head, I was planning for the worst. Hence my motto "hope and pray for the best and plan for the worst."

I am not telling you to do what I did but rather sharing my thought process and how I handled things. Each one of you know your own situation and marriage. All I am saying is, when a person is scorned, they will do unexpected things. So, keep your eyes open, your business hat on, and your heart in check. Keep in mind though that the funds in your newly opened bank account may still be subjected to equitable division in a divorce.

Tip #10: Consult a Certified Divorce Coach and an attorney. Interview at least two of each. Most will give you 30 minutes free for the first consult.

A Certified Divorce Coach is a must. I suggest finding one at the early stage of contemplating a divorce. An expert will be able to provide you with mentorship and resources to assist every step of the way. She will be part of your support system, your guide, and your cheerleader. She will put you in contact with experts such as financial planners, attorneys, and therapists, to name a few. The ultimate goal of a Certified Divorce Coach is to help you stay in control, save time, save money, save you heartache and keep you out of the court system, if possible. She will be focused on assisting you holistically with the overall state of your mind, body, and spirit. Reach out to me if you need a referral. I know someone who is an expert in this field.

If you find yourself getting to that point where you are seriously considering a divorce, before you make any decisions at all, consult an attorney. Most attorneys will give you a short consult for free, typically 30 minutes or less. My suggestion is to at least talk to two different ones. I can't stress enough the importance of having the right attorney that fits your personality as well as your budget.

Keep in mind that the attorney you choose is just that, an attorney. They are not your therapist, life coach, or best friend. When you meet with one, you need to have your ducks in a row, in other words, have everything organized. Make a list of questions. Attorneys typically charge you for every minute of their time unless you have settled on a flat rate. So don't break down and cry when meeting with your attorney. Save that for when you are with your girlfriends or when you are alone.

If you find yourself lost and not knowing where to begin with accumulating all the pertinent information that an attorney might ask, below are the most common ones:

> What are your sources of income?
> What are your total debts?
> What type of retirement accounts do you have?
> What other accounts exist?

Now that you are aware of the most common questions, find yourself either an experienced financial planner or a certified divorce financial analyst. Either one of these two people can assist you with the arduous task of gathering this information. They truly can be lifesavers and your best friends.

When I was going through my divorce, I was not a financial planner yet. I was referred to a female divorce financial analyst by a dear friend of mine. She assisted me when my whole life was crashing down. She was a Godsend! Thank you, Krys! You not only helped me survive during one of the most difficult times of my life, but you helped me make that pivot to become my best self. I will elaborate more on what she taught me in the next chapter.

CHAPTER 6

How I survived

Webster's dictionary defines survive as "to manage to keep going in difficult circumstances; to live or exist in spite of hardship." Yes, I could have continued to keep going on my own but, it was much easier and more effective with a support system. You need people you can trust and lean on to give you that hug when you need it, pray for you, watch your children for a while, or just take your mind off your current circumstances.

Also, it is helpful to set goals for yourself or what you want to achieve at the end of this painful experience called divorce. This should help keep you focused and help you survive. Just remember that everyone's circumstance is different. However, there are so many people who have been through the heartache and pain of divorce or, similarly, the death of a loved one, and they have survived. So will you!

Support System

This concept cannot be emphasized enough, especially to a woman going through a life-disrupting time. The definition is *a network of people who provide an individual with practical and emotional support.* I had the best support system.

Support systems do not happen automatically. It takes many years of cultivating and building relationships. As I tried to instill in my boys, if you have friendships that you value, you must take time to nurture them. Loyal, lifelong friends don't just happen overnight. It takes time, commitment, and empathy to solidify. Friends, family, church members, sorority sisters, neighbors, coworkers, and healthcare workers can all be a part of your support system.

I will tell you this, I could not have gotten through what I got through without God who is above all else. And my support system, they are a close second. I used the phrase quite often when raising my boys, "It takes a village".

Compartmentalize

I am a master at compartmentalizing. I'm not quite sure how this came to be, but it is definitely a blessing and a curse. Though in the case of my divorce, it was a blessing.

The day after I found out the reason my marriage was falling apart, I was a mess. My best friend told me to bring my younger boys to her house. My oldest son, if you remember, I had dropped off at K4 before confronting the *paramour*. At my friend's house, all I could do was cry. She played with, fed, and entertained my boys. I couldn't speak or eat for that matter: I just cried. Looking back, I think I was at her house for the whole day.

Shortly after that day, I decided to put on my professional business hat. I reached out to a close friend for suggestions on an attorney. She actually directed me to a divorce financial analyst first. Words do not describe how helpful that was. She was kind, compassionate, and knowledgeable. She became my mentor and role model, unbeknownst to me. This is Krys whom I mentioned in the previous chapter.

My next step was finding an attorney. As you can tell, I made a to-do list. This was so helpful and kept me focused when I had to be business-like and get stuff done. Here is where the compartmentalization comes in, I would take that business hat off and go to my best friend or another close friend's house and just cry. My best friend at the time was my source of strength and comfort. She was my rock for many years. Also, there was another close friend who would hug me immediately when we came in contact with each other, and the tears just flowed. I had no control over this. No words were spoken or even necessary, just a hug. These types of relationships, the bedrock of support systems, are priceless.

Here's a warning to you ladies who are going through a divorce right now or the death of a loved one. Be careful not to let others influence your decisions. You are the one who has to live with you. The decisions you make are yours. You won't be able to blame others later for your own decisions. So, word of advice…seek God first and always for direction and guidance. Then be still and listen. He will never steer you to the wrong direction, but others might. Not intentionally, but out of concern and love for you.

One chance to get it right

At this time in my life, I had been a stay-at-home mom for a little over five years. I was out of the workforce, but still maintained my professional skills. I methodically decided that I had one chance to get this right. I did not want to have any regrets. I wanted to be able to look at my boys one day and tell them that I did everything I could to make this work. My desire was to keep our family together but in a healthy, happy way. I also did not want to have to reopen this painful wound years later, because I had to take my ex-spouse to court for more child support. So, the motto of "one chance to get it right" stuck with me throughout my divorce.

First things first, I tried to save our marriage. I asked him if he wanted to go to a different counselor. No response. On more than one occasion I asked him if he wanted to leave me. No response. Then one day I approached him like I did that night after our counseling session when I gave him one final chance to come clean.

I remember exactly where I was standing and what I was feeling on that fateful day. I said, "I am going to ask you one more time and that's it, do you want to leave me and your three little boys to be with her?" His answer rang loud and clear. YES. That was it. I knew I would have to do the hard stuff. The next day I was off to the attorney to file for the dreaded divorce.

My goals were to keep my costs down as much as I could and come to a reasonable negotiation with my soon-to-be-ex. Also, the last thing I wanted was for this to drag on and on or to have to go to court years later. I do commend us for working things out and keeping the boys our top priority. We met maybe a total of 4 times and came up with a reasonable financial and custodial agreement. The attorney I secured was really only needed to review what we came up with. I am a numbers person, not a legal person. I could negotiate but I wanted to make sure the verbiage accurately reflected what we had decided. No mediation was necessary. No court needed, it was amicable and clean…*thank God*. My friends would say if you could have a good divorce that ours was the poster child.

Avoidance

As I mentioned, the ability to compartmentalize was a blessing and a curse for me. The blessings were, I was organized, methodical, disciplined, and determined. Well here comes the curse part. Compartmentalization to me meant keeping my emotions at bay when it came to my soon-to-be- ex. Even as I am writing about avoidance, I am doing it. This has been something I didn't even realize until now. Yes, seventeen years later, I realize that I avoided many situations and encounters with my ex. In retrospect, I think it was because my desire to keep my boys' lives normal, uninterrupted, and free of pain kept me from dealing with my own feelings. I put my feelings and healing on the back burner. I think most moms do this.

As much as I feel like I did the right thing for them and our family, I do have some second thoughts. I feel like I should have stood up to my ex more. I feel like I should have held him accountable. I'm not sure he ever realized what he had done to me and the boys. I feel like we were robbed of the family we were supposed to have -like my boys were cheated. And I feel guilty I put my boys in this situation. As you can tell a flood of repressed feelings are finally coming to a head after seventeen years. Avoidance is not healthy. It just pushes all those negative emotions down. They must be dealt with but in a controlled and safe environment. I believe there is a balance. As much as I have tried to instill that into my boys, I think I need to take my own advice. Even though I wish I had many years ago, if you are like me, please know that it is not too late.

Driving force – My boys

My boys are my world, my heart, and my everything. They were and always will be my driving force. I think that's how I was able to stay so focused and accomplish what I did. I wanted to protect them. I wanted to keep their lives as normal as possible. I wanted them to feel loved and that they had a family even if their mom and dad weren't together. In the early years of our divorce, we did a few family vacations together. We still get together for the boys' birthdays and special occasions.

Every decision I made, I would think of how this will affect my boys: the way I responded to and treated their father, how involved I was at their school and with their extracurricular activities.

Whom I dated. Whom I brought around them. How I took time for my self-care. I was trying to live by example. Show them rather than just preach to them how to live. How to handle adversity and the bumps in the road of life.

Thinking back, I would make the same decisions all over again. Although I would be remiss if I did not admit that there were times I second-guessed myself and my choices. For instance, I chose not to bring a stepdad into their lives. I did have the opportunity about three years after my divorce. I met a wonderful man and he had two children similar in age to my boys. We had fun together, all seven of us. The kids liked each other and got along. He treated me wonderfully. He was kind, loving, caring, and thoughtful. I knew I would not have to worry about infidelity.

I backed away though because his relationship with his ex was not as amicable as mine was with mine. This made me nervous. I had worked so hard to keep my life and the boys' lives drama-free. I did not want to take on someone else's drama. So, I ended it. To this day, we are still friends. Often times, I wonder the impact a loving relationship would have had on my boys. The good example and role model they would have had. Did I choose wisely? I am a firm believer that everything happens for a reason and people come into our lives for a lifetime or a particular season for a reason. But ultimately, God is in control.

You Are Not in This Alone

#6: Take small steps when suddenly single

One of my clients found herself in this situation. Her husband lost his battle with cancer at an early age. She found herself alone, scared, and unclear on how to move forward. I encouraged her to take one step at a time. That's exactly what we did...together. Shortly after her grieving, we got together and I helped her gather all her financial information. We took a step-by-step approach and did not try to handle everything at once. We established a budget, focused on paying off her debts (credit card as well as house), and set up a savings plan after her debts were paid off.

Today she is living within her budget, saving for the extra stuff in life (emergencies, vacations, etc.), and on a plan to save enough to retire earlier than she originally anticipated. Talk about becoming your best self despite tragic circumstances. I am so proud of her!

Pursuit of Your Best Self

Tip #11: Do your due diligence.

I remember thinking that my life was falling apart and that I was not really sure why. It's sad to say, but I got into investigative mode and I started snooping around. I just had to find out why and what was going on. As a matter of fact, I even turned to a private investigator. I needed some answers and my husband wasn't giving them to me. Turns out I did not need to use the private investigator as my husband finally admitted his adultery.

Well, prior to his confession when I was in my investigative mode, I reached out to a dear friend of mine. She put me in touch with a colleague of hers who was a divorce financial analyst. Like I mentioned in the previous chapter, she was a Godsend. She spoke with me for at least an hour the first time I called. The one thing that resonates louder than the other pieces of advice she gave me was making copies of all financial documents and other important papers.

Her advice was that when in doubt, you should make copies and keep them all in a safe place that only you are aware of. Below is a list of many of the items she mentioned:

- Retirement accounts
- Investment accounts
- Bank accounts/bank statements
- Mortgage papers
- Title to home(s)
- Tax returns – 3 years minimum
- Spouse's paystub or W-2s from the last couple of years
- Credit card statements
- Any other loan documents

- HELOC
- Student loans
- Personal lines of credit
- Life insurance policies
- Property & Casualty Insurance policies
- Wills & Living Wills
- If businesses are involved, then make sure you have documents such as financial statements, bank accounts, tax returns etc.
- Personal Identification: Social security cards, drivers' licenses, passports, etc.
- Logins and passwords for all online accounts
- Proof of income (paystub or W2)

Remember, every situation is different. Whenever you are looking through your financial details and you're in doubt, make those copies. This was one of the best things I did. I suggest you make those copies sooner than later. Even if you are in a happy, healthy marriage, it is so important that you know where your important financial information is at all times. Remember life happens and you never know when you might be suddenly single.

Tip #12: Consult a financial planner or divorce financial analyst.

I cannot emphasize this enough, not because I am a financial planner with a CPA, but because I know I can help you. I can make this devastating, tumultuous time in your life a bit easier. I can walk with you and be someone you can lean on, count on, and who will also hold you accountable. It doesn't make you weak or incompetent. On the contrary, it shows strength to reach out and get help when you need it; get direction when your world is turned upside down and get clarity so you can become your best self. I promise that even though this is a messy transition, it is possible to wipe the slate clean, get a fresh start, reset your future goals, and lay out a plan for the next chapter of your life.

This was what happened to me. I did it with the help of my support system. If I can do it, you can do it, too. And I would love to be the one to educate, guide, and partner with you on your journey to becoming your best self. I would love to be part of your support system. If not me, then find someone you are comfortable with who has these credentials.

CHAPTER 7

Finding myself

————••••○○ ● ○○•••————••————

How do you find yourself? And what does this process entail?

This process is different for everyone. Mine includes focusing on being a child of God before anything else, focusing on my health and well-being, and being the best mom possible to my children —I have to put this third as it is like the oxygen mask on an airplane...you must put yours on first in order to help or take care of those that you are with. The fourth and fifth are somewhat of a tie for me. That is, having no regrets and finding my balance. When I say this, it brings to mind the hero in the movie Karate Kid, where he had to find his physical and mental balance to become the best he could be at karate.

Being a child of God

Throughout my divorce, my relationship with God had grown and developed into something far more than I ever knew could exist. My desire to know Him better and have Him as a constant companion started out as a desperate need that has now turned into something that seems so natural. It's as natural as breathing, stopping to smell the roses, and marveling at a beautiful, colorful sunrise or the sheer luminescence of the moon. I do believe that He will use our lowest of lows to mold and transform us to be who He wants us to be. That, in my mind, is our best self.

Focus on your health

It didn't take me long to realize that for me to get through this life-altering event and find my power, I had to take care of myself. This was not as easy as it sounds. When your world has been shattered, picking yourself up and dusting yourself off so that you can move forward requires focus, resolve, discipline, and a motivating factor.

Now let's back up just a bit. I remember that after I found out that my husband was unfaithful, I felt so ugly. I felt old and unattractive. Keep in mind I was only thirty-seven years old. Why anyone would want to be with me was a thought that ran through my mind over and over again. I had not been eating well. Not that I didn't want to eat, just that nothing tasted good. I was not hungry. I had to force myself to eat to stay healthy enough to take care of my boys.

One day, I was looking at myself in the bathroom mirror and I did not like what I saw. A skinny, broken woman who was wallowing in self-pity was looking back at me. STOP IT! I dropped down to my knees and asked God to help me.

So many times in my life, I have tried to do things my way or on my own. Whenever I tried to do it my way or independently, more often than not, my life turned into chaos. With age and wisdom, I have learned that if I ask God for help and then surrender to Him —I mean completely surrender, He will take control. Sometimes, it turns out the way I want, other times not. Like the saying goes, "Sometimes the best result is an unanswered prayer." In time, I would see this much more clearly than I did at that moment.

It was like an audiotape playing over and over again in my head... *You must eat. You must stay healthy so you can take care of these sweet, little boys. They did not ask for this. They should not suffer because of the mistakes of their parents.*

Slowly but surely, I started getting my appetite back. It took a while and wasn't easy, but remember, I am stubborn. I felt with every ounce of my being that God put me on this earth to raise these boys. I actually could hear Him tell me that in my prayers. Not all the time, but I think He spoke whenever I needed to hear from Him the most.

Being the best mom

Being a mom and having four children had been a dream of mine for as long as I can remember. However, I wanted to dance on Broadway before becoming a mom. So I knew, even as a little girl, that I would be a mom, but it'd be later in life. I had things I wanted to accomplish. Places I wanted to go. And of course, I had to find my prince charming.

My personality is such that if I decide to do something, I endeavor to do it to the best of my ability. I want to succeed or at least give it 110 percent of what I've got. How do you give more than 100 percent? Not sure, but I heard one of my mentors say that and it stuck with me. I liked it! It was my mantra. So being a mom, the best mom, was no different.

True confession: as a married woman, well at least in the marriage I was in, I was not the best mom. I had a short fuse, and I got frustrated easily. I blamed it on being Italian but really it was my situation and how I felt about myself. Regardless, there was no excuse. These were my little boys, just babies. They didn't do anything wrong. I was just miserable. I say this to be transparent and also, to show you the power of God. I know He plucked me out of my unhealthy marriage so that I could be a better mother to my boys. The best mother I could be. There begins my mission in life, my purpose, my heart!

No regrets

This was tough. I had multiple people with various opinions sharing with me how I should handle everything. How I should handle my ex, the divorce, my life. They were not hesitant to share their ideas on how I should treat my husband, soon to be ex-husband. A couple of them even said that I should throw all his stuff out on the front lawn and burn it. I felt like I was in a tunnel, or better yet, a hole in which there were all kinds of voices echoing and talking at the same time. My head was spinning.

Once again, I went down on my knees, asking God for help. I wanted to do the right things. I wanted to make the best decisions I could, but what were they? It was a voice inside me that told me that as long as I think about how this will impact the boys before making any decisions, I can't go wrong. With this in mind then, and even to this day, that's how I made and continued to make my decisions, or at least the big ones.

My goal was to be able to look my boys in the eyes at various stages of their lives and be able to say to them that I did the very best I could. The best I could do to save my marriage. The best I could to have their lives be as normal and happy as possible given the circumstances. No regrets. Well, no more than necessary.

Finding balance

This to me is always a work in progress. I would characterize myself as an overachiever now and a perfectionist in my younger days. To my credit, I have backed off trying to attain perfectionist status since the birth of my boys. Well, probably not the first one. He got the overachiever, perfectionist mom, unfortunately. And yes, I see signs of that character trait in him. We should be cognizant of the fact that our children take on some of our desirable and not-so-desirable personality traits.

Balance, balance, balance...life is about balance. I have been preaching to my oldest especially about balancing his life. It started in high school and carries on to this day. I have tried to direct not only him but all three of my boys that a happy, healthy life requires balance: taking care of yourself, nurturing your friendships, fostering your romantic relationships, and giving back to others or your community, among other things.

I have known about balance all my life but didn't always practice it myself. It really came to a head when I was going through my divorce. I felt like I was wearing so many different hats and had so many responsibilities that at times, I just wanted to break. Sometimes I felt like I was too exhausted to handle anything else and I wasn't doing anything well. That's when balance became so much clearer to me. I did not have to do everything perfectly. I just had to figure out the right proportion and prioritize my responsibilities. Balance.

I had to find my equilibrium, my mental steadiness, and my emotional stability. Seriously, how could I teach this to my boys if I couldn't even do it myself? Total transparency…I know what balance is and for the most part, I can accomplish this. However, there are times my balance is a bit lopsided. At least I recognize it.

You Are Not in This Alone

#7: Update your beneficiaries

An acquaintance of mine whom I had not seen in a couple of years reached out to me, and I was happy and honored that she thought of doing so. She was named the Executrix of her stepfather's estate. Her mother had passed away a few years before her stepfather. Well, her stepfather did not change his beneficiaries on his qualified accounts. The beneficiary was still his deceased wife. Also, he had never requested or claimed the two IRAs that were in his deceased wife's name. She had not named any beneficiary on her IRAs. If the IRA owner fails to name one and resides in a community property state, then the spouse would be entitled to the account, as it would become part of the deceased regular estate.

In an equitable distribution approach, if the account owner doesn't name any beneficiaries and dies without a will, the IRA is subject to state "laws of intestate succession." While these vary from state to state, usually, surviving spouses and children top the list to inherit assets —including the IRA funds. (*Investopedia: Can a Spouse Not Named as a Beneficiary Receive Assets from an IRA? 12-29- 20)*

To make a long story short, it was a mess and took me and my client way longer than was necessary to get all the assets of both her mother and stepfather into an estate account where the assets could be distributed to the estate beneficiaries. When I say way longer, I am talking about what should have taken a few months — took almost a year. This all could have been avoided had her stepfather claimed his wife's IRAs whether he received them directly or they went to an estate account. Then he should have changed his beneficiaries to someone other than his deceased wife.

Unfortunately, I have multiple examples of client scenarios like this one. If you decide to take just one financial tip from this book and put it into practice, I recommend you choose *keeping your beneficiaries updated.*

In addition, make sure you have at least one contingent beneficiary listed as life is unpredictable. Be extra prepared. Remember my motto, "Hope and pray for the best and prepare for the worst."

Don't forget about your Non-Qualified or taxable accounts. These must be designated to a recipient to receive upon your passing. They are not called beneficiaries, they're called Transfer on Death recipients. As with the Qualified accounts, I strongly suggest you have a primary recipient and a contingent. I can't stress enough how much easier your financial affairs will be handled upon your passing if accounts have primary and contingent recipients or beneficiaries.

Pursuit of Your Best Self

Tip #13: Learn how joint accounts work.

There are two primary types of joint accounts: bank accounts and credit card accounts.

Joint bank accounts obviously are owned by two or more people. Each party has the right to make decisions on this account. They can deposit into or withdraw money from it. Technically, either of the parties can take out the entire amount of money in the account and close it. You're definitely not advised to do this. Remember this is a marital property and will need to be considered in the divorce negotiations. As I mentioned previously, it's best to keep things as is or maintain the status quo until the divorce is final.

This is what you can and cannot do with your joint bank account:

- You cannot take your spouse's name off the joint account without his or her permission. Even if you've banked with the same bank for years, they are not allowed to help you cut your spouse off from an asset that is legally theirs.
- If you are amicable with your soon-to-be ex-spouse, you can discuss closing the joint account and splitting the money.
- You can speak with a divorce attorney. Ask if it is legal in your state to withdraw half the contents of the account. This may only be allowed if divorce proceedings have not begun. This is why it's important to consult with an attorney.
- Last but not least, if you are concerned that your soon-to-be ex-spouse may withdraw all the money,

then you should contact the bank and let them know you are going through a divorce. Ask them to freeze your account so that neither of you can carry out transactions on it. I would advise that you contact your attorney and discuss how and when you should inform your soon-to-be ex-spouse that you put a freeze on the account. (The Ascent: Getting Divorced? Here's What Happens to Your Joint Bank Accounts. And Atlanta Divorce Law Group: Should I Open a Separate Bank Account If I Am Ready to File for Divorce?)

Joint Credit Card Accounts

The only way to close a joint credit card account is to pay off the balance and then both you and your spouse can agree to close it.

The danger of leaving your joint card open after the divorce is that you run the risk of your ex-spouse making excessive charges and running up the balance. Regardless of whether or not you are divorced, you both are still jointly responsible for the balance.

As far as the creditors are concerned, it doesn't matter to them what the divorce decree says. In their eyes, you and your ex-spouse signed a joint contract and you are both responsible for the debt.

Ways to be proactive:

- Document every deposit and withdrawal from your joint bank account.
- Save every receipt or documentation of charges on your joint credit card.
- Alert all creditors that you are going through a divorce. They may have some of their own procedures or protocol that needs to be followed.

- Remember as mentioned in the last chapter...copy copy copy. Keep copies of all statements. This will be especially helpful if your soon-to-be-ex decides to run up your joint credit card balance or take excess funds out of your joint bank account. (The Ascent: What to Do With Joint Credit Cards When Getting a Divorce?)

Tip #14: Update Will, Power of Attorney (POA), Healthcare Directive, and all beneficiary accounts.

Updating your will is so important but, it's often a forgotten step in the post-divorce process. It is important for a few reasons, which include:

- If you have minors i.e., kids, you and your spouse should work together to determine who should be the guardian in the unfortunate event that you both pass away at the same time.
- A will directs how your assets are distributed in the event of your death. But a will alone does not help avoid probate.
- It is basically your final words and wishes. (Legalzoom: 5 Ways to Avoid Probate 3-8- 2021).

Updating your Power of Attorney (POA) for your finances and healthcare is just as important. You want to make sure you appoint a person you trust to handle your finances as well as your healthcare decisions in the unfortunate event you become unable to do so. This can be a family member, a friend, or a trusted colleague. Just give it some serious consideration before making these decisions. I also advise talking with the person(s) you decide to name as POA(s).

Updating your beneficiaries should be top on your post-divorce list. Beneficiaries should be listed on your IRAs as well as employer retirement accounts such as 401k, 457 plans, and 403b. These are called Qualified or tax-deferred accounts. Not only should you name a primary beneficiary but also a contingent beneficiary. I have seen many estate settlements made much more difficult and cumbersome because beneficiaries were not updated or no contingent beneficiaries were named.

CHAPTER 8

Becoming my best self

———••••○○ ● ○○••••———

There are two things that I say to my prospective clients that resonate with me and carry into my personal life. The first one is, "I won't tell you what you want to hear but what you need to hear." The second is, "If you don't want or like tough love, then I am not the right fit for you."

I do this with myself as well, and I call it my self-talk. Sometimes it's hard to hear what I have to say to myself, but it is necessary. This has helped with my development into becoming my best self. Taking time to listen, to try new things, and to go on new adventures are just some of the advice I received from people who love and care about me along my journey and to this moment. Now I am sharing them with you.

Listening to God & my inside voice

It's true that when things are not going so well or there is trauma in my life, I pray more. Sad, I know. But it's my reality. During the summer from hell and throughout the divorce process, as well as shortly after, I prayed fervently. I studied my bible. As a matter of fact, I read it from cover to cover. Not an easy task I might add, but definitely something I would recommend. I purchased the chronological bible to accomplish this goal. It was easier for me because it read more like a story.

Once again, that summer from hell, I was at my lowest point. I am usually an upbeat, positive, happy, pleasant person to be around. Well, not for most of 2003. In my desperation, I turned to God more than ever before. The more I dug into His word and surrendered to

Him, the more I felt his presence. Remember I shared with you that I heard His voice one night. Well, it happened one other time but not quite as audible as the first one. It was during a time when my soon-to-be ex-husband invited me to come see his new house before I let the boys go over there. Yes, you guessed it; he was living there with the *paramour.*

I was driving down what seemed like an endless street on my way to his house when I broke down in tears. As I got closer, I thought, *you can't go in there like this. You are a mess.* I tried to fight back the tears and gain control but to no avail. As I got closer, I spoke to God. I told Him that I can't do this by myself and asked that He please help me. All I can say is God is amazing! As I approached the neighborhood all my tears were gone and no sign of crying was on my face.

It's hard to believe after my messy breakdown. I walked into that house like I was a realtor or at a business meeting. Compartmentalization was the key at this moment. I left there knowing that God is always with me, I just needed to recognize this and ask for His help. "Seek the Lord and his strength; seek his presence continually." Psalm 105:4

Not afraid of trying new things (both personally and professionally)

My focus was on being the best mom that I could ever be for my boys. They deserved it. It took me a while to realize that I deserve some things too, just for me, Keli. It was the spring of 2007, almost three years after my divorce was final. I was on vacation in the panhandle of Florida with some friends. As I was getting ready to go out for dinner, I was trying to find some jewelry that would go with my outfit. That's when it hit me. I had an idea for getting a traveling jewelry case that would keep my jewelry from tangling, protect it, and make it easy to find.

Then I thought, *if I needed this, there may be other women that might need it as well.* This was the beginning of my journey as an inventor. I learned so much on this journey, not only professionally but also about myself. I took the idea from concept to market. There were scary moments along the way, and moments that I wanted to give up, but my stubbornness and the support of a few important people in my life kept me going.

One scary moment was when I auditioned for Everyday Edisons. This was a show similar to Shark Tank, but on a much lower scale. I waited for about five hours to get in front of four judges. One of them was on a computer probably researching my idea to make sure it was original. The presentation lasted about five minutes which seemed like an eternity. After the audition, one of the judges followed me out of the room. He told me they are not going to put me on the show but my idea "has legs" —those were his exact words. That's all I needed to give me the push to move forward.

It was amazing how one kind person or mentor can impact your life. Unlike my dance teacher who had the opposite effect on me. My next audition was for Shark Tank. I spent almost all day outside in the cold and misty weather to get about one minute in front of a judge. Talk about the build-up of anxiety and nerves. Needless to say, I did not make it on the show. However, this did not stop me from moving forward. This venture lasted —from start to finish— about four years. It did not take off but was definitely a great learning experience as well as source of growth both professionally and personally.

In 2011, I embarked on my next venture. It had been almost seven years since my divorce was final. My boys were almost thirteen, eleven, and eight. I decided to pursue becoming a financial planner. In my former life, I was a CPA. I practiced in public and private accounting. Throughout the years when my boys were young, talking toddlers and then preschoolers, I was asked by one of my former colleagues at my private accounting job to do some part-time work. I was honored he thought of me. It was fun and gave me a personal outlet. It kept my skills sharpened as we discussed in Chapter 1. I was blessed to have him reach out to me and for his trust and confidence in me.

I always knew I wanted to go back to work one day when my boys were older. I did not want to be fifty years old and wondering what I was going to do with my life. My financial planner at the time encouraged me to think about going into financial planning. He thought it would be a great fit for me. With my accounting background, my interpersonal skills, and my desire to educate and help, it seemed like a natural fit. Of course, I prayed about it because it was a big commitment. I had five tests that I had to take as well as I had to build a client base. This takes time, lots of it.

Although my boys were young, I spoke with them about my goal and why it was important to me. I wanted them to understand and also learn from my actions.

Finding my passion

Becoming a financial planner was not easy. Trying to study for five tests and take care of three boys by myself was —in want of a better word— a challenge. I had to be disciplined, focused, and diligent about setting time aside for myself to study. Throughout this whole process, I was honest with and included my boys in my decisions. I wanted them to feel respected.

I started my new career in August of 2011. I was excited and eager to learn. Well God had another plan for me, unfortunately. My middle son had a severe eye injury in October 2011. He was on bed rest for six weeks with very little movement and obviously no school. He had to sleep while sitting up at a ninety-degree angle for three months. This was a traumatic time in our lives.

I remember it like yesterday, yet it seems like a lifetime ago. I was on my knees every day, praying for God to save his eye and heal him completely. I share this story with you to let you know how important it is to listen to God and follow His timing. This is one example of when I wanted to do something, and I took control, but God pulled me back. My heart aches for my son to this day for the fact that he had to go through this. I wished it had been me instead.

After this traumatic event, there were other times in my life that I tried to do things my way and God gave me a wake-up call. So, I learned slowly but surely that I needed to surrender to Him once again. I said to Him, "If financial planning was your will for my life, then let it be." To this day, I wake up every morning and thank God for each day, for allowing me to be in it, and then I let Him know I want to honor and glorify Him.

I believe this is what He wants me to do. I have a servant's heart and am a giver by nature. I feel like I can help others, and I have a strong desire to do so. I feel like my clients are my family, my team. I have found my passion. And I wish others could find theirs, too.

Making a difference

When I was younger, material things mattered to me. As a matter of fact, one of my signature songs was Material Girl by Madonna. I thought things could make me happy. Not only objects but that knight in shining armor. In my heart, I believe that is one of the reasons I had to experience my divorce. The loss of what I had dreamed of and imagined my life to be. I had to go through that experience to get me to where I am now —the person that God wanted me to be.

Throughout my journey, I realized I had made some mistakes for which I had to make amends. I owed an apology to several people in my life whom I felt that I had not been empathetic towards, but instead selfish. So off I went to right my wrongs. There were four people that I sought out to apologize to. It was not easy but was well worth it in the end. I told them I did not reach out for any other reasons but to say I'm sorry. All of them told me I didn't need to do that. I shared with them the spiritual journey that I had been on and this was a large piece of my recovery and obedience to God. It was awesome!

Now I felt whole. I felt like I could be empathetic and make a difference in others' lives. Part of this is being able to share my journey. One of my first steps in doing so was teaching a bible study for single moms. This was definitely a stretch for me. I did not feel like I was qualified enough to teach others God's word. I did not even feel comfortable praying in front of others at this point.

Over time, I became more comfortable teaching and praying with others. I loved my single moms' group and led this bible study for five and a half years. When my business started to grow, I had to back away and let someone else lead it. I still miss it and miss the ladies. Fortunately, however, many of them have turned into clients, and more importantly, friends.

Financial planning makes me complete. It allows me to use my education, professional experience, life skills, relationship skills, and desire to educate to help others. I want to make a difference because when I am gone, what will remain is the impact I have had on other people's lives, not just my stuff.

New Adventures

The best word I can come up with as a descriptor for this year is *Healing*. One of my reasons for writing this book is to help me with my own healing as well as to help others. If one person can learn one thing from my story, then, I'll feel like I have made a difference. I am that much closer to accomplishing the mission that I feel I was put on this earth for.

Part of my healing process is striving for balance in my life. Part of this means taking time to "pause and smell the roses." My sister told me that many years ago when I was so focused on my career and in the midst of moving to Atlanta back in 1995. I will never forget the day she said that. She even bought me a Precious Moments doll back then that had a little girl smelling some flowers. I still have this doll. She sits on my bathroom counter so I can look at her every morning as I get ready for work.

Finding my balance includes spending time taking care of myself. I exercise regularly, eat well, and try to get enough sleep. Spend quality time with my boys and close friends by having date nights, going on trips, or just having heart-to-heart conversations. Taking care of my clients and team members by giving them exceptional customer care and service and continuing to learn and grow professionally. Most important is spending time with God by doing my devotional every morning, praying throughout the day, and thanking Him for everything —the good and the bad. I also thank Him for making me the person that He wants me to be. My goal is to have more experiences and make memories with the people I love. My thought is that memories will last but stuff will just disappear.

You Are Not in This Alone

#8: Find power in the pivot

This is a much easier section to write, having been through my divorce and currently coming up on the 17^h anniversary of my divorce. The other women I interviewed seconded this comment. Most of the women have been divorced for at least five years, and a few have been for as long as I have been.

I would say all but one of the twenty women was in a much better place emotionally, spiritually, and financially. The one I would say hadn't quite let go and embraced her new life. In other words, she is still living in the past and has somewhat of a victim mentality. Remember it takes two to make a marriage work and two to make it fail. Owning your part in the demise of the marriage is a huge pivotal moment to becoming your best self. In order to make that pivot, here are some awesome words of wisdom from the women interviewed:

- Don't put yourself last. Your dreams are worthwhile. You are important.
- Listen to God or if you don't believe in God, then listen to your higher being or your inner voice. Surrender to the events that are happening and follow your gut. Your intuition is usually spot on.
- Try new things. Step outside your comfort zone and put yourself out there. The worst that can happen is you fail but, in the process, you learn so much about yourself and what you are meant to be doing, and where you are meant to be.
- Follow your passion. If you are not sure what that is anymore then take some quiet time, close your eyes and remember back when you were a little girl. What did you want to be? What did you want to accomplish? This may not be how you feel now

or something that you can reasonably accomplish but it gives you a starting point. Don't be afraid to dream.

- Think about your legacy. What do you want others to say about you when you are no longer on this planet? What kind of difference do you want to make in your children's, friends, family, and strangers' lives?
- Go on adventures. Experience new things and places. Have no regrets. Book a trip with your children, your extended family, or friends. Venture out and try different places. It doesn't have to be expensive. It can be a staycation in your own hometown. Just go to places you haven't been or do things you normally don't do. Be creative.

Pursuit of Your Best Self

Tip #15: Remaking your finances is a process.

This is the most exciting part for me to share with you. At 38, and with three children under the age of six, it was time to start remaking myself. I did not want to have to reopen this painful wound years later because I had to take my ex to court for more child support or something else. It's a bit scary but also exciting. This did not happen overnight by any means. This was, and still is, a journey, not a destination.

As a wise woman once told me, "Let's tackle this elephant one small bite at a time." And that's exactly what I did and still do today. Establishing credit in my own name was one of the first steps I took.

Below are a few items to focus on to help you build your credit score:

- Close all joint accounts after your divorce is finalized.
- Apply for your own credit card if you don't have one in your name already. Once you receive one, be sure to only put on there what you can pay off at the end of each month. Yes, there may be emergency situations such as getting new tires, fixing water heater breaks, etc., that will require you to carry a balance. Make an effort by cutting back somewhere else to pay this expense off as soon as possible. *The Balance: How to Rebuild Your Credit Score after Divorce, 6-28-2020.*
- Build an emergency fund: I recommend six months' worth of monthly expenses in an emergency fund. This may be a bit too much for you to do at first, so start with one month and build on that foundation. Remember, an emergency fund is just that — for

emergencies. Not for vacations or that new outfit you want.

- Make a budget: Most of my clients cringe when I make mention of this. If you don't like the word *budget,* then consider it as tracking your monthly expenses. When you track your monthly expenses, it's important to write down everything. Manage your source of income. Live within your means (i.e., don't spend more than you bring in). It seems like a simple concept but so many people feel like they can use their credit cards to fill the gap. Sad to say, but that was my experience growing up. That's all I knew when I went off to college. Really, that has been the way I have always lived until I met my husband. Together, we focused on paying off all our debt in our first year of marriage. What a liberating feeling!

- Save, save, save: Yes, even if it is twenty dollars per month. The reason is twofold. One, to build up your emergency fund and eventually your retirement account. Then second, to teach you discipline. My opinion on financial success and independence boils down to discipline. Do not spend more than you earn, save a specific amount consistently and invest wisely. I often ask my clients especially single moms who tell me that they can't save anything, "How often do you stop at a convenience store to get coffee?" They typically say, "Two times a week. Ok...two times a week multiplied by two dollars per coffee is four dollars per week or sixteen dollars per month give or take. My next question would be, "Do you think you can give up that coffee stop and make some coffee at home?" The answer is always *yes.* But the exciting part for me is seeing that light bulb go off in my client's head. Their eyes fill with hope and the confidence that they can do this. Talk about empowering.

- Refine your skills or learn new ones. Figure out what you are good at and what you enjoy doing, then focus on sharpening your skills. This could lead you to the career or job that you have always wanted and that you weren't initially aware of. I can't stress how important it is to take time off for yourself. Spend time growing personally and professionally so you can become your best self.

- Push yourself outside your comfort zone. Don't be afraid to try new things. My first attempt at this was in 2008, about four years after my divorce was final. I had a brilliant idea (or at least I thought I did) to invent a traveling jewelry case that kept your jewelry protected, tangle-free, and easy to access. I took it from idea to market. I had several people that God put in my path to assist me on this journey. I couldn't have done it without them. I learned so much and had fun along the way. Talk about a confidence booster, but also a humbling experience. Even though my invention never really took off, this was just one important step on my journey to becoming my best self.

- On my journey to becoming my best self, I did not want to overlook my children's own journey to becoming their best selves. I wanted to instill a sound knowledge and understanding of finances into them. And an appreciation for it as well. When my children were young, I bought three small clear containers for each of them. I labeled them Give, Save, Live. Every Friday, I paid them for chores they did around the house. When I paid them, I let them know it was up to them to decide what amount to put in each container. It was definitely interesting to see who put what in, and where. They always had to put the money in this order of priority.... Give, Save, Live. I did not make this up myself. I wish I had. I learned it from a sermon at church and then I did some investigating and found this idea. Now, at the ages of twenty-two, twenty, and eighteen, I feel like this helped them realize the value of hard work, money, and giving to others.

Conclusion

Through my journey of ups and downs, good times and not-so-good times, happiness and grief, I came out a stronger, better, and happier mother and woman. Today, I am a financial planner sharing my knowledge, experience, and emotions in an effort to help other women in similar situations. I know it sounds cliché, but I found my passion. I found the career that makes me happy and excited to go to work every day. I love helping people! I love educating, guiding, and walking with them on their journey to achieving their financial goals and becoming financially independent. I feel like this shows when I meet with a client for the first time. I have been blessed and I want to bless others by helping them. It's not about the money; it's about the impact on others' lives.

I tell prospects after our first meeting, which I have always called *Discovery meeting*, "If you come away having learned just one thing, then I have done my job; the job that God has directed me to do."

My conclusion on this is that life is a series of small and big moments that add up to your life. Make the most of each moment. I am not saying that every moment will be fabulous but feel each moment. It may be good or bad, happy or sad, full of contentment or anger, clarity or confusion, togetherness or aloneness. Regardless, embrace each feeling. Enjoy the pleasant ones, acknowledge the negative ones then let them go. Each moment is a building block that is creating your best self. As one of my interviewees said, "You can be much happier on the other side if you allow it!"

Continuing your journey with me

N ow that you have read my story and understand the journey better and gotten some tips personally and financially, what is next? You are not alone on your journey. Everyone's experience is and will be unique. There is no one answer for everyone. That is why it is so important to have the right people in place to help guide you through this time in your life. You need a support system on many levels. Your family, friends, church, and coworkers can all be your support system.

In addition to this emotional support system, you need a professional support system. Four professionals are an integral part of navigating the divorce process, and they include, an attorney, therapist, divorce coach, and financial planner. Ideally, you should team up with a Divorce Coach and Financial Planner while you are in the contemplation stage. The divorce coach can help you figure out if divorce is really necessary, and then help you navigate the process. The financial planner can help you handle your finances throughout the entire divorce process.

This is such an important time that you should not be making decisions about your financial future without the guidance of a professional. I have seen many people who have given up everything or way more than they should have because they just wanted to be done. They ended up with liquidity as well as tax issues. This is where I come in. I am the voice of reason, practical and honest. I will assist in helping you understand your new financial picture – current, during, and after your divorce.

I know you can get through this pivotal event in your life and become your best self. The next step in continuing your journey with me is to schedule your free personal consultation by going to www.CapFSGeorgia.com. We will have a confidential discussion in person, by video conference, or by phone about what you need and how I can best help you.

Here are some ways I can help navigate you through your divorce.

Pre-Divorce Services

- Educate clients about the options, processes, and financial aspects of divorce.
- Assist with organizing critical documents.
- Prepare budgets and a Statement of Net Worth (the Financial Affidavit).
- Explain the financial pitfalls to avoid during the negotiation process.
- Recommend lawyers/mediators based on the client's needs, preferences, and budget.

In the Process of Divorcing

- Review and analyze financial documents, insurance policies, and annuity contracts.
- Prepare you for meetings with your lawyer or mediator.
- Establish goals for children's college tuition.
- Discuss the need for Qualified Domestic Relations Order (QDRO).

Post-Divorce

- Provide attorney recommendations to prepare new legal documents including the Will, POA, Health Care Directive, Trusts, etc.
- Evaluate and update the monthly budget.
- Provide recommendations for new experts including CPAs, P&C insurance, Health insurance, realtors, etc.
- Assist with obtaining new insurance coverage (Life, P&C, Health, and Long-Term Care).

- Review your credit score/report and advise you on how to improve your credit rating.
- Help with the transfer of assets.

The goal is to have a plan for you that focuses on getting you in a healthy position personally and financially. Remember, getting through your divorce or, any traumatic event, is a step-by-step process that takes time. When taking care of yourself and your family becomes critical, I am here to support, educate, and guide you towards a secure reset of your financial future.

Things to remember

————•••○○ ⬤ ○○•••————

Credit Report

- A credit report is a detailed summary of an individual's credit history, prepared by a credit bureau.
- Reports include personal information, details on lines of credit, public records such as bankruptcies, and a list of entities that have asked to see the consumer's credit report.
- The three major credit bureaus—Equifax, Experian, and TransUnion—are each required to provide consumers with one free report each year.

Credit Utilization

The credit utilization ratio is the percentage of a borrower's total available credit that is currently being utilized. The credit utilization ratio is a component used by credit reporting agencies in calculating a borrower's credit score. Lowering the credit utilization ratio can help a borrower to improve their credit score. (Investopedia, Credit Score)

Freeze Accounts

- A frozen account is a bank or investment account through which no debit transaction can be made.
- Account freezes are normally the result of a court order and, in some cases, they may be done by the bank itself.
- When a bank account is frozen, it may be because of money owed to another individual or business.

- Account freezes are not permanent, and generally require certain actions from the account holder before they can be lifted.

Marital Assets

- Marital property refers to property that a couple acquires during their marriage.
- Where a couple lives determines the laws that govern the distribution of marital property in the event of divorce.
- In common law property states, property that is acquired by one spouse is considered their sole property unless the title or deed carries both spouses' names. Nine states are community property states, where marital property acquired during the marriage is owned by both spouses equally. These include Arizona, California, Idaho, Louisiana, Nevada, New Mexico, Texas, Washington, and Wisconsin. (Investopedia, Common Law)

Property Transfers

The federal tax law provides that certain property transfers, including transfers between spouses and transfers "incident to divorce" — meaning that the transfer occurs within one year after the end of the marriage, or is otherwise related to the divorce — are income tax-free. In general, transfers made within one year of divorce are presumed to be related to the divorce.
https://www.bnymellonwealth.com/articles/strategy/ making-tax-smart-property-transfers-in-divorce.jsp

Alimony

- Alimony refers to a periodic pre-determined sum awarded to a spouse or former spouse following a separation or divorce.
- The goal of alimony is to provide spousal support in order that they continue the lifestyle to which they are accustomed to after the divorce.

- Alimony will often be awarded to ex-spouses of long-term marriages (i.e. greater than 10 years) and will stop upon death, remarriage, or court order.
- Refusing to pay or not keeping up to date with alimony payments may result in civil or criminal charges for the payer.
- For the receiver, alimony payments have often been considered to be taxable income by the IRS; for the payer, they have been a deductible expense. However, The Tax Cuts and Jobs Act (TCJA) put forth by the Trump administration eliminated the tax deduction for alimony paid for divorce agreements executed after Dec. 31, 2018. Under the new rules, alimony recipients will no longer owe federal tax on this support. (Investopedia, Alimony)
- Alimony should not be confused with child support.
- Note that neither alimony nor child support payments may be discharged in bankruptcy.

QDRO

- During a divorce, you will not be expected to pay taxes on the immediate division of retirement accounts as long as you file them correctly with the courts.
- QDROs, or Qualified Domestic Relations Orders, manage the division of retirement accounts that are not IRAs. Division of IRAs is classified as a transfer incident to divorce. Clarifying the two is an important distinction.
- It is often the best course of action to hire a financial expert to assist in the division of assets.
- It can be easy to overlook, but make sure to update your beneficiaries during the divorce.
- QDROs resemble transfers incident to divorce in that they are tax-free transactions as long as they have been reported correctly to the courts and the IRA custodians. The receiving spouse may roll QDRO assets into their own qualified plan or into a traditional IRA. Any transfer from a qualified plan pursuant to a divorce settlement that is not deemed a QDRO by the IRS is subject to tax and penalty.

Capital Gains

- Selling a capital asset—for example, stocks, bonds, precious metals, or real estate—for more than the purchase price results in a capital gain.
- Short-term capital gains result from selling capital assets owned for one year or less and are taxed as regular income.
- Long-term capital gains result from selling capital assets owned for more than one year and are subject to a tax of 0%, 15%, or 20%.

Custodial Parent

There are many factors involved when making child custody decisions. When determining the home in which to place the child, the court strives to reach a decision in "the best interests of the child." Judges typically focus on the viewpoint of the child as opposed to what the parents want. Each child custody case is unique and different. However, some key factors are always taken into consideration. They include:

1. The Parent-Child Relationship
2. Lifestyle and Conduct of the Parents
3. The Parents Mental and Physical Health
4. The Parents Ability to Provide for the Child
5. Continuity with the Primary Caregiver
6. The Child's Established Pattern (home, school, religion)
7. The Preference of the Child
8. Child's age, gender, and Mental and Physical Health

If none of these factors clearly favor one parent over the other, the court will focus on which parent can provide a stable environment for the children. When younger children are involved, custody is usually awarded to the parent who has been the child's primary caregiver.

https://www.lawfirms.com/resources/who-gets-custody-of-the-children-in-a-divorce.html

Claiming Children as Dependents

Only one person can claim a child as a dependent during the same tax year, which means both parents cannot do so, including those who are divorced. In the case of divorce, the parent with whom the child resided for the majority of the tax year can make the claim. If both parents get equal time during the tax year, the parent with the highest adjusted gross income (AGI) can make the claim.

The child tax credit is worth up to $2,000 for the 2020 tax year, for those who meet its requirements. Having dependent children may also allow you to claim other significant tax credits, including the earned income credit (EIC). Together, the tax savings are substantial for many American families.

The child tax credit is phased out at higher income levels. The credit is reduced to zero in stages as income rises above $400,000 on joint returns, and above $200,000 on single and head of household returns.

If you didn't qualify in prior years, recheck your eligibility each year so you don't miss out on this tax break.

As part of the American Rescue Plan Act of 2021, the child tax credit cap has been increased to $3,000 in 2021 for those between six and 17 years old, and $3,600 for those under six. The credit is also now fully refundable. The credit now starts to phase out at the following income levels: $75,000 for single filers, $112,500 for heads of households, and $150,000 for married couples filing jointly.

Certified Divorce Coach

A divorce coach is someone who can help you navigate the muddy waters of your divorce and help you move on with your life more easily.

Below are eight ways a divorce coach can help you through your divorce:

1. Save money

Using a divorce coach can help you save money. How? When you use a divorce coach, they can help you work through your options and discover the best pathway for you before you start paying costly legal fees.

As they can provide emotional support, they can be sounding boards for you when you need to vent about your ex – and it will be way cheaper than paying your lawyer in 6-minute blocks to listen!

2. Stay Calm

A divorce coach can be there for you when times get stressful and you feel like you're starting to lose control either of the situation or emotionally. They will be there for you when you need them and will help you stay calm throughout the process.

3. Gain Clarity About Your Options

By talking through all your available options with someone who is not emotionally involved in your divorce, you will be able to gain clarity around what options are available to you and help you narrow down which would be best for you and your family.

4. Prepare for Mediation or Court

With the right experience, a divorce coach can help you prepare for divorce mediation or court appearances. If they're certified and have the relevant training and experience, their help can be invaluable to make sure your mediation or legal issues are dealt with quickly and as amicably as possible.

5. Be an Emotional Support

Often when people get divorced, they don't want to burden their friends or family with their emotions. A divorce coach can be a pillar of support for you during this time. They're completely independent and can help you work through your emotions without having to feel forced to 'pick a side'.

6. Improve Your Co-Parenting Skills

Until you go through a divorce, you'll likely have zero skills when it comes to co-parenting. As someone who works with divorcing parties on a daily basis, I have learned that a divorce coach can help you navigate co-parenting with grace and ease.

7. Set Goals

A big part of divorce is what happens afterward. Yet so many people fail to recognize this and after their divorce is completed, they may feel at a loss for how to move forward and live successfully. A divorce coach can help you work out what goals you should be setting for your future along with realistic timeframes to achieve them.

8. Make Your Transition Easier

In a nutshell, divorce coaches can help you transition from separation to divorce as painlessly as possible. That's not to say it won't be a painful experience – of course, divorce is never easy and emotionless. But having someone alongside you for the journey to keep you on the right path can be immensely helpful.

If you're thinking of hiring a divorce coach, make sure you check what qualifications and experience they have. As with any coaching, it's important to know that the person you hire is fully trained and compliant with any legal bodies in your state.

https://moveon.com.au/what-is-a-divorce-coach-do-you-need-one/

Financial Planner

A financial planner is a qualified investment professional who helps individuals and corporations meet their long-term financial objectives. Financial planners do their work by consulting with clients to analyze their goals, risk tolerance[1], and life or corporate stages, then identify a suitable class of investments for them. From there they set up a program to help the client meet those goals.

Financial planners may also specialize in tax planning, asset allocation[2], risk management, and retirement and/or estate planning.

Qualified Accounts

The most common types of qualified retirement accounts are IRAs and 401(k)s. IRS guidelines determine eligibility and affect your deposits and withdrawals from such accounts. These plans allow you to contribute money in a tax-favored manner and proactively save for your retirement. In addition to deferring income taxes on any accumulation within the account, you may also receive tax breaks for the years you make contributions.
https://finance.zacks.com/non-qualified-investment-accounts-vs-qualified-accounts- 1347.html

Non-qualified accounts

A non-qualifying investment is an investment that does not qualify for any level of tax-deferred or tax-exempt status. Investments of this sort are made with after-tax money. They are purchased and held in tax-deferred accounts, plans or trusts. Returns from these investments are taxed on an annual basis.

Wills

- A will is a legal document that spells out your wishes regarding the care of your children, as well as the distribution of your assets after your death.
- Failure to prepare a will typically leaves decisions about your estate in the hands of judges or state officials and may also cause family strife.
- You can prepare a valid will yourself, but you should have the document witnessed to decrease the likelihood of

successful challenges later.

- To be completely sure everything is in order, consider having your will prepared by a trust and estate attorney.

Notes

[1]**Risk tolerance** is an investor's general ability to withstand risk inherent in investing. The risk tolerance questionnaire is designed to determine your risk tolerance and is judged based on three factors: time horizon, long-term goals and expectations, and short-term risk attitudes. The adviser uses their own experience and subjective evaluation of your answers to help determine your risk tolerance.

[2]**Asset Allocation** does not guarantee a profit or protect against a loss in a declining market. It is a method used to help manage investment risk.

Power of Attorney

- A power of attorney allows one person to give legal authority to another person to act on their behalf.
- A financial power of attorney authorizes an individual to make financial decisions, while a medical power of attorney allows for someone to make medical decisions.
- In some cases, a financial power of attorney can be used for isolated, one-off situations where it is not convenient for you to be present.
- Financial and medical powers of attorney should be in separate documents and can be designated to the same person or two different individuals.
- Generally, both a financial power of attorney and medical power of attorney must be signed before a notary public.

Healthcare Directives

- A healthcare power of attorney (HCPA) is a legal document that empowers a specific individual to speak with others and make decisions on your behalf concerning your medical condition, treatment, and care.

- It is important to trust your HCPA, as that person may be charged with making life-and- death decisions on your behalf.
- Although an HCPA is easy to put in place, states have different rules and forms; so, you'll need to consult those of the state in which you live.

Tax-Deferred

Tax-deferred status refers to investment earnings—such as interest, dividends, or capital gains— that accumulate tax-free until the investor takes constructive receipt of the profits. Some common examples of tax-deferred investments include individual retirement accounts (IRAs) and deferred annuities.

Emergency fund

- An emergency fund is a financial safety net for future mishaps and/or unexpected expenses.
- Emergency funds should typically have three to six months' worth of expenses, although the pandemic has led some experts to start suggesting up to one year's worth.
- Individuals should keep their emergency funds in accounts that are easily accessible and easily liquidated.
- Savers can use tax refunds and other windfalls to build up their funds.

Statement of Net Worth

- A personal financial statement lists all assets and liabilities of an individual or couple.
- An individual's net worth is determined by subtracting their liabilities from their assets— a positive net worth shows more assets than liabilities.
- Net worth can fluctuate over time as the values of assets and liabilities change. Personal financial statements are helpful

for tracking wealth and goals, as well as applying for credit.
- Although they may be included in a personal financial statement, income and expenses are generally placed on a separate sheet called the *income statement*.

Trust

- A trust is a fiduciary relationship in which a trustor gives another party, known as the trustee, the right to hold title to property or assets for the benefit of a third party.
- While they are generally associated with the idle rich, trusts are highly versatile instruments that can be used for a wide variety of purposes to achieve specific goals.
- Each trust falls into six broad categories: living or testamentary, funded or unfunded, revocable or irrevocable. https://www.investopedia.com/terms/t/trust.asp

References

"5 Ways to Avoid Probate." 8 3 2021. *Legalzoom*. https://www.legalzoom.com/articles/5-ways-to-avoid-probate.

"Can a Spouse Not Named as a Beneficiary Receive Assets from an IRA?" 29 12 2020. *Investopedia*. https://www.investopedia.com/ask/answers/05/inheritira.asp.

Caplinger, Dan. "What to Do With Joint Credit Cards When Getting a Divorce?" 13 9 2019. *The Ascent*. https://www.fool.com/the-ascent/credit-cards/articles/what-to-do-with-joint-credit-cards-when-you-get-a-divorce/.

"Credit Score." 11 3 2021. *Investopedia*. https://www.investopedia.com/terms/c/credit_score.asp.

Divorce, Hello. "Who Gets Custody Of The Children in a Divorce?" 2021. *LawFirms*. https://www.lawfirms.com/resources/who-gets-custody-of-the-children-in-a-divorce.html.

"Divorced or Separated and Income Taxes." 17 11 2021. *E-File*. https://www.efile.com/divorce-or-separated-and-taxes/.

Epstein, Lita. "Marriage vs. Common-Law Marriage: What's the Difference?" 21 9 2021. *Investopedia*. https://www.investopedia.com/financial-edge/0210/marriage-vs.-common-law-what-it-means-financially.aspx.

Gambone, Gregory. "Non Qualified Investment Accounts Vs. Qualified Accounts." 2021. *Zacks*. https://finance.zacks.com/non-qualified-investment-accounts-vs-qualified-accounts-1347.html.

George, Dana. "Getting Divorced? Here's What Happens to Your Joint Bank Account." 3 10 2020. *The Ascent*. https://www.fool.com/the-ascent/banks/articles/getting-divorced-heres-what-happens-to-your-joint-bank-account/.

"How to Improve Your Credit Score." n.d. *Experian*. https://www.experian.com/blogs/ask-experian/credit-education/improving-credit/improve-credit-score/. 18 12 2018.

"How to Rebuild Your Credit After Divorce." 28 6 2020. *The Balance*. https://www.thebalance.com/how-to-rebuild-your-credit-after-divorce-960366.

Kagan, Julia. "Alimony Payment." 8 9 2021. *Investopedia*. https://www.investopedia.com/terms/a/alimony-payment.asp.

—. "Trust." 19 10 2020. *Investopedia*. https://www.investopedia.com/terms/t/trust.asp.

"Making Tax-Smart Property Transfers in Divorce." 2021. *BNY Mellon Wealth Management*. https://www.bnymellonwealth.com/articles/strategy/making-tax-smart-property-transfers-in-divorce.jsp.

Ray A. Knight, CPA, J.D. and Lee G. Knight, PhD. "Tax Considerations When Dividing Property in Divorce ." 1 4 2013. *Journal of Accountancy*. https://www.journalofaccountancy.com/issues/2013/apr/20126248.html.

Shann, Ian. "What Is A Divorce Coach & Do You Need One?" 28 11 2019. *Move On*. https://moveon.com.au/what-is-a-divorce-coach-do-you-need-one/.

"Should I Open a Separate Bank Account If I Am Ready To File For Divorce?" 2021. *Atlanta Divorce Law Group*. https://atlantadivorcelawgroup.com/blog/should-i-open-a-separate-bank-account-during-a-divorce/.

References

Williams, Rebekah. "The Long Term Asset Issue ." 27 5 2020. *Garofalo Law Group.* https://glgfirm.com/divorce-the-long-term-asset-issues/.

Made in the USA
Columbia, SC
12 August 2023

21430891R00068